Cambridge Elements ≡

Elements in Language Teaching
edited by
Heath Rose
Linacre College, University of Oxford
Jim McKinley
University College London

MEDIATING INNOVATION THROUGH LANGUAGE TEACHER EDUCATION

Martin East
The University of Auckland

T0328766

CAMBRIDGE
UNIVERSITY PRESS

Shaftesbury Road, Cambridge CB2 8EA, United Kingdom

One Liberty Plaza, 20th Floor, New York, NY 10006, USA

477 Williamstown Road, Port Melbourne, VIC 3207, Australia

314–321, 3rd Floor, Plot 3, Splendor Forum, Jasola District Centre, New Delhi – 110025, India

103 Penang Road, #05–06/07, Visioncrest Commercial, Singapore 238467

Cambridge University Press is part of Cambridge University Press & Assessment, a department of the University of Cambridge.

We share the University's mission to contribute to society through the pursuit of education, learning and research at the highest international levels of excellence.

www.cambridge.org
Information on this title: www.cambridge.org/9781009124263

DOI: 10.1017/9781009127998

First published 2022

A catalogue record for this publication is available from the British Library.

ISBN 978-1-009-12426-3 Paperback
ISSN 2632-4415 (online)
ISSN 2632-4407 (print)

Mediating Innovation through Language Teacher Education

Elements in Language Teaching

DOI: 10.1017/9781009127998
First published online: November 2022

Martin East
The University of Auckland
Author for correspondence: Martin East, m.east@auckland.ac.nz

Abstract: This Element examines how pedagogical innovation in language classrooms can be mediated through language teacher education (LTE) by subjecting the author's own practices as a teacher educator to scrutiny. Starting from the premise that implementing innovation can be a challenging enterprise, effective LTE is framed as being built on helping practitioners to recognise and confront often deeply rooted beliefs and adjust subsequent practices through critical reflection on what an innovation may look like both theoretically and practically. A critically reflective lens is then applied to the author's own work as a teacher educator over several years through a research approach known as self-study of teacher education practices or S-STEP. The approach highlights changes to the author's beliefs and practices as lessons emerged from beginning teachers' engagement with innovative ideas. These are presented with the aim of better understanding how teachers' beliefs and practices with regard to innovation can be enhanced effectively.

This Element also has a video abstract: www.cambridge.org/meast

Keywords: language teacher education, innovation, reflective practice, S-STEP, task-based language teaching

ISBNs: 9781009124263 (PB), 9781009127998 (OC)
ISSNs: 2632-4415 (online), 2632-4407 (print)

Contents

1 Mediating Innovation through Language Teacher Education

In their introduction to an edited volume that documented the implementation of innovations in English Language Teaching in a range of contexts across the globe, Hyland and Wong (2013) wrote, '[c]hange seems to be a constant in our professional lives as teachers' (p. 1). They hereby underscored two important realities with regard to innovating pedagogical practice: there is no avoiding change; and change management resides primarily in the hands of classroom practitioners.

Implementing pedagogical innovation can be an exciting enterprise. Griffiths (2021) noted, 'with the exception only of the learners themselves, teachers are by far the largest contributors to variance in achievement' (p. 1). Also, teachers do generally want to be effective and to create powerful quality learning experiences that will make a positive difference for their students (see, e.g., Van den Branden, 2009a, and Burns, 2010, with regard to language teachers and Bergmark et al., 2018, and Perryman & Calvert, 2020, more widely). Taking these perspectives into account, many teachers may be open to innovation and willing to try out new ideas with a view to potentially enhancing students' learning outcomes.

Implementing pedagogical innovation can also be a tricky business. As innovations begin to be implemented, there are other forces, including elements of tradition, that, for a variety of reasons, can exert strong influence. In some cases, teachers may be openly resistant to innovation because, as Hyland and Wong (2013) put it, '[n]ot all teachers are ready for change' (p. 2). More experienced teachers in particular may present arguments against change in words such as 'we've always done it like this' (see, e.g., Snyder, 2017).

Writing with regard to the complex interplay that seems to persist between innovation and tradition in a broad range of educational contexts, Tocci et al. (2019) wrote:

> chalkboards gave way to whiteboards that are giving way to smartboards, on which teachers broadcast information to students sitting in tablet desks that supplanted wooden desks once bolted to the floor. And at the end of a series of such lessons, students will likely show that they have learned this information by answering multiple-choice questions, no longer on a quiz or scantron form but on a laptop accessing a Web-based proprietary learning management system. (p. viii)

Tocci et al. (2019) concluded, '[e]very innovative practice is implemented within the constraints and opportunities of our educational histories' (p. viii). Or, in words attributed to Jean-Baptiste Alphonse Karr back in 1849, *plus ça change, plus c'est la même chose* – the more things change, the more they stay the same. There remains a persistent struggle between innovation and tradition.

From a theoretical/methodological standpoint, the teaching and learning of additional languages (L2) has been the subject of innovation over several decades. Under the banner of so-called Communicative Language Teaching (CLT), pedagogical practice has, theoretically, moved on from the widely established but strongly teacher-led grammar and accuracy-focused methods represented primarily by grammar-translation and audio-lingualism. In their place has come what Brown (2014) referred to a 'turn-of-the century wave of interest' in more learner-centred pedagogies that, in his view, has brought about three key shifts:

1. language has come to be seen as 'interactive communication among individuals, each with a *sociocultural identity'*
2. teachers are now perceived to be 'treating the language classroom as a locus of meaningful, authentic exchanges among users of language'
3. L2 learning is constructed as 'the creation of meaning through interpersonal negotiation among learners' (p. 206).

As will be made clear later in this Element, the momentum towards change in L2 pedagogy actually predates Brown's (2014) turn-of-the-century claim. Even so, Brown has captured the essence of learner-centred innovation. Gone, it would seem, are the days of 'chalk and talk' and 'drill and kill' in the L2 classroom. Nonetheless, writing in the specific context of the innovations in L2 pedagogy that appear to have been inspired by Brown's shifts in emphasis, Van den Branden (2009a) made a critical point. He argued that, despite moves towards innovation, teachers are (literally or metaphorically) 'still standing in front of a group of students with a piece of chalk in their hand' (p. 659). Notwithstanding strong advocacy over several decades for more learner-centred and experiential approaches, teachers' practices in L2 classrooms may continue to be very teacher-led and expository.

The past few years provide a particularly unique example of attempts to innovate and the tendency to push back. From very early in 2020, and as a consequence of COVID-19, education as we know it was substantially overturned on an unprecedented scale. Across the globe, a great deal of teaching and learning was suddenly pivoted from face-to-face to online, and many teachers found themselves compelled to revolutionise their practices. Using technology to enhance L2 teaching and learning is not in itself innovative (see, e.g., Blake, 2011), and enrolments into dedicated online L2 courses is growing. Nevertheless, prior to the disruptions caused by COVID-19, most L2 learning was still facilitated face to face in classrooms, and the sudden move to online, often made at speed and with limited support and resources, was perceived by many as an abrupt (and not necessarily welcome) response to an emergency situation (see, e.g., Strickler, 2022). In the words of Moser et al. (2020), emergency remote teaching 'is not, and cannot be, the same as planned online teaching' (p. 2).

Although it is too early to provide a comprehensive evaluation of the extent to which innovations precipitated by the pandemic were successful and will be sustained longer term, Moser et al. (2020) went on to suggest that, especially in such unexpected and often insufficiently supported circumstances, L2 teachers may return to practices that, from a learner-centred perspective, undermine a communicative and interactive approach to L2 learning – that is, they may 'revert to low-quality drills, reduce learners' exposure to and use of the target language, and rely on easy-to-find activities devoid of meaning' (p. 12).

Is innovation always doomed to resistance, painstakingly slow progress, and a return to the status quo? Not necessarily. Teachers may well be, as Griffiths (2021) identified, the principal contributors to variance in students' success. Teachers also represent 'the major source of *controllable* variance' (Hattie, 2012, p. 149, my emphasis). This assertion would suggest that innovating teachers' practices can potentially be achieved with suitable mediation. This is arguably where *teacher education* comes in.

The purpose of this Element is to consider language teacher education (LTE) as a crucial mediating component in helping language teachers to embrace innovative practices in L2 classrooms. It arises from my own many years of experience working (and talking) with teachers of languages, principally at the pre-service (beginning teacher) level. More particularly, in this Element I consider what I have learned about facilitating innovation as I have reflected on my experiences in and of LTE, in particular with beginning teachers.

The *context* in which I have mediated innovative practice is with teachers in New Zealand, and with specific regard to the introduction of a revised national curriculum for schools – the New Zealand Curriculum or NZC – mandated from 2010 (Ministry of Education, 2007). Across all subject areas, this revised curriculum reflected and carried forward a momentum to encourage a shift from a traditional top-down teacher-led pedagogical approach to a more innovative bottom-up learner-centred teaching and learning model. In turn, teacher educators have had to consider their models of teacher preparation and support in light of curricular drivers.

The *phenomenon* through which I have mediated innovative practice with teachers of L2 is so-called task-based language teaching (hereafter, TBLT), a learner-centred and experiential approach to L2 pedagogy that stands in contrast to more established and outmoded teacher-fronted grammar-based approaches. In the context of *Learning Languages*, a new curriculum area within the NZC, the reform has initiated strong encouragement, at the level of New Zealand's Ministry of Education, for teachers to consider TBLT as one means of fulfilling curricular expectations. Nonetheless, and despite a history of development dating back to the 1980s, TBLT is perceived by many across the world as 'still a relatively recent innovation' (Long, 2016, p. 28). Shifting teachers' practices towards a more task-based approach is not necessarily straightforward.

A few caveats to present at the start. This Element is about:

1. innovation in L2 teaching through the example of TBLT, but not principally about TBLT itself (see Jackson, 2022, for this)
2. my work as a language teacher educator, but not purely about language teacher educators, who they are and what they do (see Barkhuizen, 2019, for an exploration of language teacher educator identity)
3. my reflections on pedagogical effective practice at the levels of the L2 classroom and the LTE space, but not primarily about teacher reflective practice (see Farrell, 2021, in that regard).

This Element therefore builds on aspects of others that have been published in this series, but takes their arguments in a new direction. Barkhuizen (2019), for example, noted a paucity of focus on the *teacher educators themselves* in the scholarship around LTE. He cited Peercy et al. (2019) who argued, '[w]e currently know relatively little about teacher educators as *learners* and as *reflective scholars* open to examining *their own practice and research*' (p. 2, my emphases). This Element provides the space and opportunity for me to step back from what I did over a decade of work in school-level LTE, and to take a self-reflective look back at that work. I thereby consider and evaluate what seemed to work and what seemed less successful and draw some conclusions about practice as 'a *learner* of LTE' (Peercy & Sharkey, 2020, p. 106, my emphasis). What I present here may therefore be framed as a *self-study of teacher education practices* or S-STEP – a study approach that focuses on the self as the central player in the effectiveness of teacher education.[1]

It should be acknowledged at the outset that, just as innovations in teaching practice may often be hindered by the influence of traditional thinking and practices, S-STEP as a methodology stands as innovative in comparison with more established research approaches. S-STEP is not yet considered a mainstream or widespread methodological paradigm, at least not in the field

---

[1] The acronym S-STTEP is increasingly found in the literature. It denotes the addition of *teaching* alongside teacher education. Following Peercy and Sharkey (2020), I use S-STEP in this Element, but I could equally have used S-STTEP.

of LTE. As Rose (2019) put it, it is a kind of research that 'has yet to make a major impact in language teaching research' (p. 901). This Element takes some steps to address and to close that gap, but is, in itself, an experiment in innovation and a somewhat risky enterprise. Nevertheless, I see this enterprise as appropriate for what I would like to achieve in an Element whose focus is on mediating innovation through LTE. My overarching goal in this contribution to the series is to address the complex issue of facilitating pedagogical innovation among beginning teachers via initial teacher education (ITE), through my own retrospective reflections on my own work as a pre-service language teacher educator.

1.1 The Aim and Organisation of This Element

This Element has five main sections:

1. In this first section, I introduce the topic of innovation in language teaching and the focus of this Element on myself and my own practices as a language teacher educator. I go on to present the essential tension in practice that underpins innovation in classrooms – teacher-led contrasted with learner-centred – and consider what this tension means for developments to L2 pedagogical practice. Using TBLT as an example of innovation, the section concludes with an overview of four contexts across the globe where attempts have been made to innovate practice through TBLT, as well as the challenges that have emerged.

2. The focus of the second section is on LTE and a consideration of two key elements that I argue must be taken into consideration for LTE programmes to be successful – teacher cognition and reflective practice. I go on to relate these two key elements to S-STEP as a means of enabling me as a teacher educator to take account of my own beliefs about effective pedagogy and effective LTE alongside critical reflection on my own practices as a teacher educator.

3. Section 3 introduces the New Zealand context which is the focus of the LTE work that is presented in this Element. The section takes a look at what I did as a language teacher educator working with pre-service teachers of languages by presenting background information on the case in question. I briefly describe my initial two years in ITE (2008–2009) and the core aspects of my work at that time. I include an overview of the qualification within which I worked as a teacher educator and the LTE course that was a key component of this qualification. I incorporate a brief description of a preliminary in-depth investigation (2010–2011) that gave impetus to initial amendments that I made to the course (2012). I introduce these amendments,

including the teaching as inquiry model that underpinned the reflective practices of the course participants and the coursework that was aligned to the teaching as inquiry approach.

4. Section 4 provides brief accounts of four different studies that I undertook in the course of a six-year period (2012–2017), alongside several changes that I made to my own practices during that time as a consequence of reflecting on the cumulative evidence I was collecting. A crucial component of this descriptive overview and outline of changes to practice is the presentation of four short vignettes, one from each study. Each vignette is designed to provide illustrative dimensions of the data that I collected during the six-year period and that formed the essential sources for my reflection on my own work as a teacher educator and how that work might need to change.

5. The final section, Section 5, discusses the findings of the longitudinal research, summarises my developing practices as a language teacher educator during this time, and relates these to S-STEP. I use this discussion to consider the implications for future LTE. A concluding section summarises my own developments as a language teacher educator and LTE researcher.

1.2 Innovating the Classroom – from Teacher-Led to Learner-Centred

Griffiths (2021) argued that there was a time in history when the teacher was seen as 'the unquestioned fount of all knowledge . . . and source of authority'. She continued, 'it could probably be said that for centuries, if not millennia, *teacher-centred* was the educational norm' (p. 1, my emphasis). Griffiths named the ancient Chinese philosopher Confucius as one representative of the top-down, teacher-led pedagogical model. In light of its considerable historical precedence, this approach where the teacher is seen as the *sage on the stage* is very entrenched in teachers' thinking and practices. It is arguably often perceived as *the* way to manage effective teaching and learning in classrooms.

A contrasting learner-centred educational model can also be traced back many centuries. The so-called Socratic method, which utilises collaborative argument and dialogue through posing and answering questions to encourage critical thinking and comprehension, owes its name (if not its genesis) to the Greek philosopher Socrates. In a more learner-centred approach, the teacher becomes the *guide on the side*, drawing out from learners their own thinking and understanding.

It seems, then, that two contrasting philosophical approaches to effective teaching and learning have been around for an exceptionally long time. In recent times, the teacher-led approach has been informed by a behaviourist theory of learning, a psychological theoretical perspective that was particularly influential in the 1940s and 1950s, principally in the United States. From a behaviourist perspective, the teacher represents the expert who stands at the front of the class and delivers knowledge to students. The students' role is passively to receive the knowledge the teacher imparts. This knowledge will subsequently be tested in summative ways.

Beginning in the 1960s, however, debates about effective teaching and learning began to shift educationalists' thinking away from a behaviourist stance to a standpoint informed by social and experiential theories of learning. Very early significant contributors in the development of a learner-centred approach had been the American psychologist John Dewey (1859–1952), the Swiss psychologist Jean Piaget (1896–1980), and the Soviet psychologist Lev Vygotsky (1896–1934). The challenge to behaviourism emerging in the 1960s was further influenced by the theorising of Jerome Bruner (1915–2016) who was highly influential in the development of learner-centred and 'discovery learning' focused curricula (e.g., Bruner, 1960, 1966, 1973).

From a social/experiential or *constructivist* perspective, the teacher moves into the role of facilitator, working with individuals and groups of learners whose own role is actively to seek out knowledge and understanding for themselves through their own inquiries, and as they engage in interaction with others. Group work and collaborative learning may be central components, and assessments may be more embedded into the teaching and learning process.

It would seem that both pedagogical approaches (top-down and bottom-up) have considerable historical precedent. That said, a student-focused pedagogical approach may be perceived by many as a *newer* or *improved* way to manage effective teaching and learning in comparison with a teacher-centric model (e.g., Schweisfurth, 2013). Weimer's (2013) summary of a range of studies led her to conclude that, when compared with findings from teacher-led classrooms, there existed 'a convincing commendation of learner-centered approaches . . . [which] promote a different, deeper, and better kind of learning' (p. 33).

The move to learner-centredness is all very well in theory. Several major problems have arisen in practice. One crucial problem is that the shift to learner-centredness has been contested by some theorists and researchers.

Kirschner et al. (2006), for example, concluded from an analysis of a range of studies that research supporting a learner-focused approach was lacking. They argued that, on the contrary, evidence from controlled studies 'almost uniformly supports direct, strong instructional guidance rather than constructivist-based minimal guidance' (p. 83). Citing Kirschner et al., Coe et al. (2014) argued that a social/experiential approach 'is not supported by research evidence, which broadly favours direct instruction'. Coe et al. went on to assert, 'if teachers want them [learners] to learn new ideas, knowledge or methods they need to teach them directly' (p. 23).

It should be noted that the arguments put forward by Kirschner et al. were disputed (see, e.g., Hmelo-Silver et al., 2007; and Schmidt et al., 2007). It should also be noted that the constructivist classroom is not a 'a teacher-free zone' where group work and discovery learning 'work their effect without any need for mediation' (East, 2012, p. 82). The teacher remains vital to the classroom endeavour. Indeed, Griffiths (2021) argued that, despite an apprehension that learner-centred pedagogies may have made teachers effectively redundant, 'here we still are!' (p. 1).

The ongoing importance of teachers in the educational endeavour raises the second critical problem of a shift to learner-centredness – that it has been resisted by teachers in many contexts. That is, from a pedagogical perspective a struggle persists between constructivist learner-centred ideas and a traditional behaviourist-informed perspective on teaching and learning that has dominated classroom practices for many years. In this sense, therefore, constructivism in education, and all that this means for educational practice, remains innovative.

The clash between innovation and tradition, at the levels of both theory and practice, creates a highly complex situation in which teachers might try to put pedagogical innovation into practice. In what follows, I consider what all this has meant for the L2 classroom.

1.3 Innovating the Language Classroom – Communicative Approaches

Rose (2019) identified the communicative movement of the 1970s that gave rise to CLT as the most recent major attempt at innovation in L2 classrooms. In my own writings, I have often drawn on Benson and Voller's (1997) description of the advent of CLT because I regard it as a succinct and to-the-point portrayal of what was happening at the time of its emergence. They wrote:

> From time to time, a new concept enters the field of language education as an alternative method or approach, but rapidly grows in significance to the point where it comes fundamentally to condition thinking throughout the field. Such was the case with Communicative Language Teaching ... which began life in the late 1960s as an alternative to 'structural' and 'grammar-translation' models of teaching, but rapidly became an axiom of language teaching methodology. The question ceased to be, 'Should we be teaching languages communicatively?', and became, 'How do we teach languages communicatively?'. As part of this paradigm shift, other concepts

(authenticity, learner-centredness, negotiation, etc.) began to cluster around a 'communicative' core. (p. 10)

Benson and Voller's (1997) positive portrayal of the advent of CLT belies significant tensions in practice. Citing Medgyes (1986), Rose (2019) noted that CLT was met at the time with strong resistance among teachers. Medgyes had argued that what seemed to be needed in the communicative classroom was 'a teacher of extraordinary abilities' who 'above all ... must be *learner-centred*'. Medgyes went on to refer to learner-centredness in what can be construed as somewhat scathing terms – it was, in his words, 'the great gimmick of today' and 'tagged on to every single language-teaching approach, method, methodology, procedure, and technique, communicative and non-communicative alike' (p. 107).

As Rose (2019) revisited Medgyes' (1986) arguments, he drew the conclusion that it seemed that the attempt at innovation heralded by CLT was being imposed in a top-down way on the basis of researchers' claims about what was effective pedagogically, without attempts to engage teachers in the discussion. As a consequence, Rose noted that uptake of CLT was relatively slow. Furthermore, a teacher-led version of CLT, which became known as the 'weak' model, has persisted over many years. By the 1980s, weak CLT had become 'more or less standard practice' (Howatt, 1984, p. 279). It is, furthermore, a practice that continues to find expression in contemporary L2 classrooms.

One example of practice that has persisted into the present is the very familiar classroom sequence of Presentation/Practice/Production, or PPP. Put simply, in the PPP sequence, the teacher (as expert) first explains a grammatical principle to the class in a direct, teacher-led way. Then, the students practise the targeted rule through different kinds of grammar practice exercise (such as fill in the gap with the correct grammatical form; match parts of sentences together; transform a series of sentences from one grammatical form to another – e.g., active to passive, present to past). Finally, the students utilise the rule in some kind of communicative activity (e.g., a role-play to practise buying food and drink in a café). In the traditional PPP classroom, there is limited (if any) focus on creative use of language, and limited (or no) opportunity to use language beyond the confines of the practised rule.

PPP remains quite entrenched in the teaching and learning of languages in many contexts, arguably because it represents a straightforward, and tried and tested, instructional sequence. It has, for example, been central to LTE programmes such as the Cambridge Certificate in Teaching English to Speakers of Other Languages (CELTA). However, a stronger emphasis on more constructivist pedagogies has witnessed several changes to practice in the L2 classroom and has precipitated what many would regard as exciting and powerful opportunities for effective learning to occur (e.g., the three changes to practice I cited earlier from Brown, 2014). At a minimum, a shift from teacher-led to learner-centred has given rise to more open and creative communicative activities in the Production stage of a PPP lesson.

More particularly, a shift towards more learner-centred approaches has given rise to language teaching and learning approaches such as TBLT. The 1980s witnessed the emergence of TBLT as a communicative approach that has continued the push towards learner-centredness, in particular as a contrast to the teacher-dominated practices of weak CLT or PPP. That is, TBLT is built on an educational philosophy that sees 'important roles for holism, experiential learning, and learner-centered pedagogy' and on constructivist theories of learning that encourage 'the interactive roles of the social and linguistic environment in providing learning opportunities, and scaffolding learners into them' (Norris et al., 2009, p. 15). The central construct of TBLT is the task itself as something that language learners carry out for themselves (see, e.g., Jackson, 2022).

Despite the potential of TBLT to realise a communicative agenda in learner-centred and experiential ways, TBLT remains not part of the mainstream. As Ellis (2018) expressed it, TBLT (at least in its most experiential forms) 'can conflict with teachers' and learners' beliefs about language, leading at best to doubts and at worst to rejection of TBLT' (p. 274). Bygate (2020) put it in this way: TBLT has yet to live up to its aspiration and potential as 'a free-standing approach to second language education', endorsed by all those who have a stake in the language teaching and learning endeavour. There remains, therefore, 'a fundamental challenge in translating the TBLT project from research and theory to the widespread practice that its proponents claim for it' (p. 276). Taking into account that, forty years after its emergence, TBLT remains 'a contested endeavour' (East, 2017b), this makes TBLT a useful example of the tensions that emerge between innovation and tradition, paving the way for a consideration of where LTE comes in.

1.4 Contexts Where TBLT Has Been Introduced – to Greater or Lesser Effect

In East (2021a), I considered, for illustrative purposes, five contexts across the globe where, in one way or another, innovation with regard to TBLT has found some traction but has also met with resistance from tradition. These illustrate attempts to implement TBLT ideas at the school level, alongside outcomes of different evaluations into their success (see also Jackson, 2022, for other contexts in which TBLT ideas have been influential, to varying degrees of success). In what follows, I briefly summarise the key challenges I presented with regard to implementing innovation in four of these contexts – India, Belgium, Hong Kong and China. (I present the fifth context – New Zealand – later in this Element.)

1. The Bangalore Communicational Teaching Project in South India (1979–1984) represented a grassroots or bottom-up process to initiate innovation with a view to improving school-aged learners' acquisition of English as L2. The innovation was implemented as a reaction against prevailing teacher-led grammar-oriented practices. The project arguably characterises the first documented attempt to innovate practice through learner-focused tasks. Problematic in practice was that the innovation was essentially driven by one advocate in particular – N. S. Prabhu (see, e.g., Prabhu, 1982, 1987). Also, most of the teachers who became involved in the project were not the regular teachers in the schools. They were, rather, more highly qualified, recruited explicitly for the project, and, as a consequence, already had a level of commitment to its success. It seems that the regular teachers were sometimes less engaged and more likely to revert to more traditional practices as the project progressed. Thus, a bottom-up attempt to innovate was confounded by teachers who arguably demonstrated insufficient buy-in to the innovation and increasingly resorted to practices with which they were more familiar.

2. A contrasting top-down initiative, primarily for those learning Dutch as L2, was commissioned by the Flemish government in the early 1990s as 'a large-scale test case for the implementation of task-based language education' (Van den Branden, 2006, p. 13). A particular focus was on adult immigrants and their children. There was a strong emphasis on supporting teachers through professional development and resources. Evidence from ongoing evaluations indicated that teachers demonstrated openness to the innovation, and valued TBLT due to its motivational emphasis on functional and academic proficiency in the target L2. However, studies revealed that, in practice, teacher implementation was variable (Van den Branden, 2009b). In particular, what teachers believed about effective pedagogy influenced what they did with TBLT ideas in their classrooms. For example, taking the resources presented to them, teachers tended to 'modify task scenarios . . . in countless ways' (p. 281). Tasks, it seemed, became 'highly flexible and kneadable material that can take on different existential guises as it passes through the minds, mouths and hands of different persons making use of it'

(Berben et al., 2007, p. 56). This autonomy to mould tasks to the context is not in itself problematic (see, e.g., East, 2017b). It becomes a challenge to innovation, however, when the tasks are essentially 'detaskified' (Samuda, 2005), that is, lose the essential criteria that originally made them tasks. In particular, it seemed that some teachers worried about their lessons being 'out of control' if they did not maintain a central position in what happened in class.

Two top-down initiatives in an Asian context – Hong Kong and mainland China – reveal challenges in practice as the encouragement to innovate came up against the more traditional practices of teachers influenced by a Confucian Heritage Culture.

3. In Hong Kong, a range of curriculum documents over a number of years has officially endorsed TBLT in the school sector (Curriculum Development Council, 1997, 1999, 2002, 2007). Over time, TBLT became quite deep-rooted as the 'core conceptual framework for the curriculum' (Adamson & Davison, 2003, p. 28). It appeared, at least superficially, that Hong Kong was 'responding positively, proactively and deeply to contemporary theorising around effective language pedagogy' (East, 2021a, p. 159). Carless (2012) asserted, however, that '[t]he reality at the chalk-face revealed . . . different issues to the more idealized picture presented in curriculum guidelines' (p. 349). A top-down approach to innovation showed itself to be ambitious in practice because, in the context, it 'challenges traditional conceptions of good teaching and learning' and 'contradicts long established pedagogic practices and community attitudes' (Adamson and Davison, 2003, p. 28).

4. In China, the National English Curriculum Standards (e.g., Chinese Ministry of Education, 2011) have drawn attention to TBLT at primary and secondary levels. Although no pedagogical approach has been mandated, TBLT is encouraged, and supported through prescribed textbooks. However, research in the Chinese context has revealed that TBLT implementation has been hindered in practice (Luo & Xing, 2015; Xiongyong & Samuel, 2011; Zhang, 2007; Zheng & Borg, 2014). Limiting implementational factors included teachers' lack of knowledge about TBLT, inadequate professional development opportunities, and negative washback from a grammar-oriented testing culture (see, e.g., Liu & Xiong, 2016; Ruan & Leung, 2012).

The challenges teachers have encountered in both Hong Kong and China appear to be common in other Asian countries (see, e.g., Tran et al., 2021, for a sociological explanation of why teachers might keep to more established ways of teaching in the context of innovation). As Lai (2015) put it, research in Asia has indicated 'a slow uptake of TBLT in classrooms', and has also 'highlighted areas of incompatibility between TBLT and the particularities of the Asian contexts so far investigated' (p. 23). It would seem that top-down initiatives to encourage innovation in Asia are having less than optimum impact, particularly where traditional language teaching methods remain popular. Once more, the teaching approaches that teachers are more used to have influenced and limited innovation.

One area of practice that illustrates the pull of established tradition is the teaching of grammar. From a constructivist-oriented learner-focused perspective, it may be theorised that grammar is best attended to by giving learners opportunities to discover and notice for themselves how grammar works as they engage collaboratively in communicative interaction. Part of the argument here is that 'if the students can work out the rule for themselves, then they are more likely to remember it' (Ur, 2012, p. 81). In the Bangalore case, for example, it was anticipated that grammar would be attended to implicitly through students' noticing of patterns in the input to which they were exposed. Beretta (1986) drew attention to one teacher who, as the project progressed, admitted that she gave extra grammar coaching to weaker students in her class. Likewise, in Hong Kong, interview data from teachers and teacher educators indicated that direct grammar teaching was regarded as 'a major teacher priority' (Carless, 2009, p. 55).

Indeed, Larsen-Freeman (2015) noted that, regardless of context, grammar instruction does not seem to have been influenced that much by research-informed findings that might align themselves with a more learner-centred approach. She argued that, by contrast, the grammar focus 'remains traditional for the most part, with grammar teaching centered on accuracy of form and rule learning, and with mechanical exercises seen as the way to bring about the learning of grammar' (p. 263). Savignon (2018) made exactly the same point. She observed that teachers 'remain adamant about explicit attention to form through practice drills, completion of textbook activities, and grammar practice worksheets'. She went on to explain why this might be the case – '[l]ong-held professional values and beliefs and specific instructional rituals often reflect how teachers themselves have been taught' (p. 7). Her words echo those of Van den Branden (2009a), whose claim regarding the forces that work against innovation (which I stated towards the start of this Element) was based on the recognition that teachers 'teach in the way they themselves were taught, and show strong resistance towards radically modifying the teaching behavior that they are so familiar with' (p. 666). L2 teachers, from this perspective, may be hindrances to innovation because they bring with them into their classrooms beliefs about what is effective pedagogically that are shaped by their own early experiences.

Each of the above cases highlights the reality recognised by Hyland and Wong (2013), that 'the stages through which innovation might move can be messy, with reinterpretations and additions made along the way' (p. 2). These may be made as accommodations to, for example, individual and contextual beliefs and preferences. It is also very clear that teachers are an indispensable component in the success (or otherwise) of innovation. Thus, irrespective of the impetus from which an encouragement to entertain TBLT as innovation is occurring (bottom-up or top-down), teachers, it seems, have a central role to play (East, 2021a; Van den Branden, 2016). Long (2016) concurred that, in comparison with the work of the teacher in the more traditional teacher-led (e.g., PPP-oriented) classroom, the more facilitative role of the teacher in TBLT is more crucial and requires greater expertise. This, Long maintained, is potentially problematic because 'large perceived differences between current performance and that required by new developments' operate as 'a major factor mitigating against teacher buy-in and adoption of new ideas' (p. 28).

Arguably an indispensable part of the answer with regard to helping teachers to implement innovation is *teacher education*. From that perspective, it is important to consider those issues that may contribute to maximising the effectiveness of LTE initiatives.

2 Teacher Education as the Vehicle for Pedagogical Innovation

Earlier in this Element, I presented the arguments that teachers have a central role to play in effective teaching and learning and are significant contributors to variance in student achievement (Griffiths, 2021), and that their contributions are 'controllable' (Hattie, 2012). In this light, the challenges emerging from attempts to innovate create a fundamental mediating role for teacher education with regard to innovating practice.

Brouwer and Korthagen (2005) suggested that what was necessary for successful teacher education were 'integrative approaches' where 'student teachers' practical experiences are closely linked to theoretical input'. These, they suggested, would 'strengthen graduates' innovative teaching competence' (p. 156). In other words, for teacher education to have any opportunity to be successful in enhancing the implementation of innovation, it needs to hold two tensions in balance: what *theory and research* say about the *benefits* of the innovation in question, and what *real classroom encounters* raise about its *challenges*.

It is not simply a question of presenting a rosy or idealistic picture of what the innovation might do which, when put to the test in real classrooms, is found wanting and is subsequently abandoned. It is a question of teachers visiting and revisiting the innovation in theory in ways that are intertwined with attempts to put the innovation into practice. This cyclical theory-practice process is under-pinned by two components of the teaching and learning enterprise that arguably make a substantial difference to the successful implementation of innovation – *teacher cognition* and *reflective practice*. I see these as two crucial elements that must consequently be taken into account if a cyclical approach to teacher education to mediate innovation is to have an opportunity for success and is to help navigate the complex environments in which innovative pedagogical approaches are being encouraged or enacted.

2.1 Teacher Cognition

Borg (2003) early defined teacher cognition as what teachers think, know and believe. Teachers bring this cognition with them into teacher education pro-grammes. As I stated at the start of this Element, in essence and for the most part teachers (whether beginners or more experienced) want to learn how to be effective practitioners and to pass on their own knowledge and understanding to a new generation in the most helpful ways (see, e.g., Burns, 2010; Van den Branden, 2009a). When aspiring teachers first enter an ITE programme, it can often seem that they embark on their studies and explorations with excitement, openness and enthusiasm. Similarly, when established teachers enter into teacher professional learning and development (PLD), this can often be because they want to refresh their practice and try out something new, and they would like an opportunity to explore how innovative practice may be implemented. However, it may not take long before clashes begin to emerge between the ideas being presented to them in LTE programmes and their own thinking and beliefs about effective pedagogy.

Teacher cognition also has a significant impact on pedagogical practice. Borg (2019) argued that teachers do not operate as 'mechanical, programmable implementers of instructional programs'. He suggested on the contrary that teachers influence classroom events as 'active decision-makers' (p. 1151). As I have put it elsewhere (East, 2021a, 2022), what teachers *think* and *believe* about what constitutes pedagogical best practice will have a substantial influ-ence on what they elect to *do* in their own classrooms. Several factors shape what teachers believe, and consequently what they will go on to do.

Firstly, teachers' beliefs may be strongly influenced by teachers' own early experiences as learners – a point forcefully made by Van den Branden (2009a) and Savignon (2018), whom I cited earlier. Furthermore, teachers' own early learning experiences may have been (indeed, most likely would have been) as passive recipients of their own teacher's expert knowledge, with the teacher being very much the one in control, and the students practising the taught knowledge in quite structured ways. These early experiences will have formed foundational beliefs regarding pedagogical effective practice. In some cases, the practices novice teachers encountered may have been unsuccessful for them, and they might seek to change their own practices in that light. In other cases, what they experienced may have worked, and worked well, for them. In these scenarios, these formative experiences may become a blueprint for future action, influencing choices regarding innovation or tradition.

Secondly, early formed beliefs can become filters that continue to play a significant role in teachers' thinking and practice even as teachers are confronted with different ideas during their ITE. That is, by the time a teacher begins an ITE programme, beliefs formed at an early stage can have become quite entrenched, resistant to change, and hard to shift. Indeed, these beliefs may have greater influence on initial classroom practice than teacher education.

Thirdly, it is well recognised that actual practice in classrooms shapes teacher development. It is not simply a question of teachers sometimes holding doggedly onto prior beliefs that have been created by their own early learning experiences. In the day-to-day life of teaching, teachers are required to make choices about practice, and several of the contextual factors they encounter may conflict with innovative ideas with which teachers may be confronted in teacher education programmes. A range of contextual factors will play a part in shaping teachers' evolving perspectives. These include the ethos of the educational establishment they are working in, expectations imposed by the working environment and other colleagues, events that take place in class, dealing with individual learner differences, and the influence of assessment (see, e.g., Coe et al., 2014). When it comes to the implementation of innovation, it is in the everyday realities of the classroom that the rubber really hits the road.

The phenomenon whereby local school contexts influence teachers' thinking and practices, and work against the implementation of innovations to which teachers may have been introduced, was described by Brouwer and Korthagen (2005) as occupational socialisation. It seems that 'during and immediately after their preservice programs, teachers experience a distinct attitude shift that entails an adjustment to teaching practices existing in schools' (p. 155). Zeichner and Tabachnick (1981) described this phenomenon as innovative ideas being 'washed out' by actual experience.

In practice, therefore, there can frequently be a misalignment between the innovative ideas that student teachers have been exposed to in their ITE and the issues they face in their day-to-day teaching environments. That is, teachers are 'influenced in powerful ways by a range of personal, physical, sociocultural, and historical milieus which interact, in both remote and immediate ways, to shape who teachers are and what they do' (Borg, 2019, p. 1154). In East's words (2021a), teachers' pedagogical choices 'will be influenced by what seems to work and what seems not to work in their own classroom contexts' (p 176).

What I have outlined above illustrates that teacher cognition plays a crucial role in teachers' pedagogical actions and choices. Furthermore, with regard to innovation this role may be hindering rather than helping. There is nonetheless evidence to suggest that, where teachers' beliefs are addressed within teacher education programmes, new understandings can be successfully established (Borg, 2003, 2011, 2015; Cabaroglu & Roberts, 2000; Ha & Murray, 2021; Richards et al., 1996). However, if those new understandings are to shift practice in the direction of innovation, I believe a second element of teacher education is important – reflective practice.

2.2 Reflective Practice

Reflective practice (see, e.g., Farrell, 2021) is represented in the moments when teachers are confronted with what they think, know and believe (their cognition) in ways that might influence a different kind of pedagogical practice. Arguably a central means of establishing new understandings, especially in beginning teachers, is critical reflective practice as 'an essential element of professional "becoming" in the journey of a teacher's development' (Brandenberg & Jones, 2017, p. 260). Williams and Grudnoff (2011) conceptualised reflection as a *process* whereby teachers improve their teaching as they consider and analyse what they actually do in classrooms. If such reflection is to improve teaching, and if it is to be successful in sustaining innovation, it needs to take into account not only the *theoretical* ideas and concepts with which teachers may be confronted in their teacher education programmes, but also classroom teachers' *real and contextually embedded* experiences. That is, teachers need to be confronted with new ideas in theory, and they also need space to try out these ideas in real classrooms. In East (2014), I identified three components that, taken together, might achieve a meaningful cyclical theory-practice interface – reflection for-in-on action.

1. Reflection-*for*-action (Killion & Todncm, 1991) represents *future-focused* reflection, both before and after a specific teaching cycle has begun. Particularly when innovations to practice are being considered, this dimension of reflection has a central role to play. Importantly, this kind of reflection provides the space for *theoretical* perspectives to be explored, ideally

outside of the classroom where teachers may have space to think about what those perspectives might look like in the classroom. Reflection-for-action is therefore a vital point of departure in the process of encouraging innovation, and a space for teachers to plan what they are going to do in their classrooms, whether in a single lesson or in the course of several lessons. Critically, it enables teachers to 'step outside of their own definitions of the world and see new perspectives' (Davis, 2005, p. 18).

However, a contextual reality (which experienced teachers know only too well) is that planned learning activities often do not go according to plan. Inevitably, changes and deviations to the plan become necessary as teachers confront and adapt to what is actually happening in their classrooms. Drawing on Schön's early influential work (Schön, 1983, 1987), I argued in East (2014) that, in the process of undertaking a particular lesson, two components of reflective practice, both of which embed critical reflection *within* actual practice, become necessary: reflection-*in*-action and reflection-*on*-action.

2. Reflection-*in*-action represents the reflection that a teacher carries out *during* a lesson which may result in immediate changes to practice. As a component of reflection-in-action, teachers need to be encouraged not to *react uncritically* to deviations to what they planned to do. Rather, they should be encouraged to develop skills in *responding critically* to what is happening, thereby making informed decisions about what to do in the face of what is happening. In other words, a knee-jerk reaction may be to abandon any attempts to innovate when a planned innovative action seems to meet with lack of success. A more measured response may well involve a change of direction, or the temporary abandonment of an activity or process that appears not to be working. However, a considered response will park the innovation for later contemplation, or reflection-*on*-action.

3. Reflection-*on*-action represents the reflection that a teacher undertakes *after* a lesson which may result in subsequent practice changes. Teachers need to be encouraged, as a component of reflecting on the actions they have taken in class, to take time out after the lesson, to think back on what happened, and thereby to make *informed* decisions about what to do next in light of what occurred.

Ideally, reflection for-in-on action becomes a cycle of critical reflective practice as part of teachers' everyday activities. When it comes to mediating innovation, the cycle of reflection enables challenging and innovative ideas to percolate through to the realities of the classroom, and to inform real-time and subsequent decisions about practice. This three-component approach to reflection is therefore one means to connect theory with practice, a connection that is an essential element of mediating innovation. Reflection for-in-on action facilitates the kind of integration that Brouwer and Korthagen (2005) had argued was a crucial element of effective teacher education. For the cycle to work with regard to innovation, the innovative ideas need to be held in the forefront of teachers' thinking as they engage in the three components.

In summary, what I have argued thus far is that effective teacher education, in particular teacher education that is going to support shifts in teachers' practices towards innovation, requires a recognition and inclusion of two critical elements:

1. Firstly, it is important to recognise that, over the years, teachers will have developed their own beliefs and understandings about pedagogical effective practice, and that they will bring these beliefs and understandings with them into a teacher education programme. These beliefs (i.e., their cognition) will be shaped not only by their prior learning experiences but also by the day-to-day realities they encounter in their places of work (both in and beyond the immediate context of their own classrooms).

2. Secondly, and in view of the beliefs and understandings that teachers bring with them, it is important to provide frequent opportunities for teachers to reflect on their experiences. These reflections need to be on both theory (e.g., what a particular innovation might look like in the classroom) and practice (e.g., what a particular innovation actually looks like in the classroom, at least at a particular point in time). Furthermore, these reflections need to be *critical* – that is, not just dismissing what does not seem to work but, rather, thinking through, and drawing conclusions about, what is actually happening in the classroom, bearing in mind theory about effective practice. This should not be seen as the work of a moment. Rather, it is an evolving process of considering (and reconsidering) theory alongside practice, taking the influence of prior beliefs into account.

2.3 S-STEP

If teacher cognition and critical reflective practice are to form the bedrocks of both effective teaching practice and effective teacher education, I would argue that it is also incumbent upon teacher educators to reflect on their own practices *as teacher educators* in light of their own beliefs about effective practice. After all, those of us who serve in the role of teacher educators are also subject to the influence of beliefs about best practice which may be framed not only by our own encounters on our journeys towards becoming teacher educators but also by defensible theoretical arguments about effective pedagogy with which we may have engaged as researchers. Each of these dimensions needs to be subjected to scrutiny in the face of unfolding experience. With particular regard to developing a fuller appreciation of what goes on specifically within LTE, Peercy and Sharkey (2020) suggested that we need 'a deeper understanding of the teacher educator as scholar, as practitioner, as researcher' (p. 106). In their view, the methodological framework that has come to be known as S-STEP – a framework that 'employs "traditional" qualitative data sources ... as well as less common data sources ... to explore questions about one's practice' (p. 106) – would provide access into that deeper understanding.

Peercy and Sharkey (2020), among others, traced the origins of S-STEP to the early 1990s, when it emerged as an organised field of educational research, validated in 1993 with the foundation of the Self-Study of Teacher Education Practices Special Interest Group (SIG) of the American Educational Research Association (AERA). They went on to argue that, since then, S-STEP has 'gained increased visibility and legitimacy in general teacher education research and scholarship' and has 'produced a robust literature and a growing influence on the field' (p. 107).

Indeed, around the time of its emergence, Zeichner (1999) acknowledged self-study as 'the single most significant development ever in the field of teacher education research' (p. 8). Building on this argument, Tidwell et al. (2009) noted that self-study constitutes 'research that could potentially have the greatest impact on teacher education and the transformation of practice' (p. xiii) – not only our own practice, but also the practice of those we work with. This is because self-study research is 'about the problems and issues that make someone an educator', creating an inescapable responsibility to 'seek to improve the learning situation not only for the self but [also] for the other' (Bullough & Pinnegar, 2001, p. 17).

Loughran (2005) identified 'an overarching need for teacher educators to pay attention to their own pedagogical reasoning and reflective practice' (p. 9). Thus, in addition to creating opportunities for beginning teachers to engage in critical reflection, self-study can be viewed as 'a pedagogic practice that enlists reflection ... in order to enable teacher educators to explore and explicate their practice ... [and] in order to improve their practice and contribute to the conversation in research on teaching and teacher education' (Hamilton & Pinnegar, 2014, p. 139).

In particular, from the perspective of the teacher educator, critical self-reflection challenges status quo thinking based on prior beliefs whereby, as Hamilton and Pinnegar (2014) put it, 'we need to only produce and reproduce the routines and practices we have already learned to enact' (p. 139). Hamilton and Pinnegar argued that, by contrast, teacher educators must put themselves in a position to 'seek out, understand, and enact emerging and evolving practices that take into account new content knowledge, new understandings of learning, and new ways of teaching, and to produce scholarship that contributes to the refinement and evolution of such knowledge' (p. 139).

According to Hamilton and Pinneger (2014), self-study research enables this positioning. For me as a language teacher educator, self-study provides a means of investigating and reflecting on *my own* beliefs and practices from *my own* perspective – that is, what *I* believed, what I subsequently *did*, and how *reflection* on what I did (in light of my students' reception of that) challenged and changed my own beliefs and subsequent actions as a teacher educator. I turn now to an introduction of the New Zealand context in which my reflective work as an ITE teacher educator was situated.

3 Introducing the New Zealand Case

The attempt to implement TBLT as innovation in New Zealand provides an interesting comparison with the other contexts I introduced earlier. Its implementation emerged neither in a bottom-up way as teachers reacted to more traditional teacher-led and grammar-focused approaches, nor as a result of a top-down mandate. Rather, TBLT was *encouraged* (but not specified or required) as a realisation of published expectations of the revised curriculum, the NZC. That is, TBLT was not specifically mentioned in the curriculum document. However, its use as one means to realise curricular aims was implicit in the wording of a newly introduced learning area, *Learning Languages,* that 'puts students' ability to communicate at the centre' through processes whereby 'students learn to use the language to make meaning' (Ministry of Education, 2007, p. 24). Subsequent teacher education initiatives more overtly supported the use of TBLT (see, e.g., East, 2012, pp. 62, 208).

However, the lack of direct exhortation in New Zealand to implement a particular pedagogical approach has meant that teachers are free to interpret a curricular L2 focus on communication however they choose. From the perspective of introducing TBLT as innovation, I commented in East (2021a) that '[o]n the positive side, teachers who wished to explore TBLT were able (indeed, encouraged and supported) to do so. On the negative side, teachers who did not wish to consider TBLT ideas could bypass them quite easily' (p. 164). As a consequence, a focus on communication in L2 classrooms is interpreted and enacted in a range of ways, both innovative and traditional.

Despite the reality of 'eclecticism in practice' (East, 2021a, p. 164), a crucial issue for me as an *ITE teacher educator* at the time of the release of the NZC was how to encourage TBLT in the context of curricular reform. At the same time, a vital concern for me as an *educational researcher* was to collect and examine the evidence for how effectively TBLT could be encouraged through LTE. Bullough and Pinneger (2001) argued that many researchers do not undertake their research in a disinterested or dispassionate way; they are, rather, 'deeply invested in their studies, personally and profoundly' (p. 13). My commitment to longitudinal research in the area of effective mediation of TBLT as innovation was born of a genuine commitment, both to my own professional practice as a teacher educator and to the professional practices of the L2 teachers I was interacting with. Before going on, in Section 4, to present dimensions of this longitudinal research and what it meant for me as a language teacher educator as the findings unfolded, in what follows I present a largely descriptive account of the ITE programme in question, and the *Teaching Languages* course for which I was responsible in the programme, as the context for my own journey as a language teacher educator.

3.1 The ITE Programme

3.1.1 Background

My work as a teacher educator responsible for the preparation of beginning teachers of L2 was situated within a one-year ITE programme – the Graduate Diploma in Teaching (Secondary). I began working in the programme in 2008.

The broader programme encouraged a reflective and inquiring approach to teacher development. Participants were expected to take account of theory about, and research into, effective pedagogical practices, and to evaluate the relevance of this theory and research for positive student learning experiences. Half of the programme was devoted to adolescent development and learning, both in theory (25 per cent) and in actual classroom practice (25 per cent). The remaining half was devoted to curriculum studies across two subject areas (major and supplementary). Students who wished to become teachers of an L2 were required to enrol in a one-year course, *Teaching Languages*, taught by me (25 per cent of the programme). This course focused on principles of effective teaching, learning and assessment of L2 (the focus of Semester 1 was on teaching and learning, with assessment considered in Semester 2). Additionally, students had to enrol in at least one year-long language specialist course (e.g., *Teaching Chinese; Teaching French*), worth 12.5 per cent, as well as a course in the supplementary curriculum area (12.5 per cent). The language specialist courses were mainly delivered by external tutors who were usually practising teachers in schools, where the principles explored in *Teaching Languages* could be applied in language-specific contexts.

To facilitate the anticipated strong theory-practice interface, the programme ran for thirty weeks (2 × 15-week semesters) and interwove time on campus with time in schools. Two school placements (seven weeks in duration), one in Semester 1, and the other in a different school in Semester 2, began and concluded with several weeks on campus (see Figure 1). During the weeks on campus, up to six hours of classroom time was available each week for the principal curriculum specialist courses like *Teaching Languages*. The on-campus times framed the in-school experiences and enabled ongoing reflection and dialogue as beginning teachers moved into and out of working in schools.

Participants in the *Teaching Languages* course included first language speakers of English who had received their education in New Zealand, and had studied a language at tertiary level. Participants were also heritage language speakers or first language speakers of their chosen principal target language (Chinese, French, German, Japanese or Spanish).[2]

When I first began my ITE work in 2008, L2 pedagogy in New Zealand's schools was largely influenced by a traditional weak CLT approach. Quite detailed and prescriptive language-specific curriculum documents had been published over a number of years to support teachers with their work in the context of an overarching curriculum framework (Ministry of Education, 1993). The earliest of these were released in 1995 (Ministry of Education, 1995a, 1995b) and the latest in 2002 (Ministry of Education, 2002a, 2002b). The documents reflected a traditional and hierarchical model of language acquisition, with suggested communicative functions, grammatical structures and vocabulary at progressive levels of complexity. These documents, and a broader consideration of the CLT principles that informed them, formed the basis of much of my LTE work in *Teaching Languages* in the first few years. The core text I chose to underpin the course was *How Languages are Learned* (Lightbown & Spada, 2006).[3]

The publication of the revised NZC for schools (Ministry of Education, 2007), mandated from 2010, became a significant catalyst for educational change. In the two years leading up to the mandatory enactment of the revised curriculum in schools (i.e., in 2008 and 2009), I familiarised myself with what the revised curriculum required and how that might be translated to teachers' work. As part of this, I volunteered to be a facilitator at a one-day workshop for L2 teachers (one of many that were arranged at the time – see Hipkins, 2010) so

---

[2] The course also included, based on demand, teachers of Samoan and Latin.
[3] Subsequent editions (4th in 2013 and 5th in 2021) have been published.

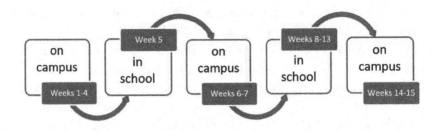

Semester 1: March-July, Weeks 1-15

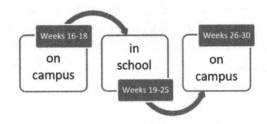

Semester 2: July-November, Weeks 16-30

Figure 1 The shape of the year (general pattern)

that I could gain first-hand experience of working through the implications of the revised NZC with practitioners. This workshop included a particular focus on using tasks, with a specific task-based resource provided for participants to work with (see East, 2012, p. 61 for a description).

As a consequence of the reform, the prescriptive curriculum documents were officially withdrawn and were no longer to be used as the basis for curricular planning. In their place was a more open-ended and non-prescriptive brief curriculum statement (Ministry of Education, 2007, pp. 24–25), alongside the encouragement for teachers to consider learner-centred approaches such as TBLT (see, e.g., Ministry of Education, 2017, 2021). This was a significant departure from previous practice.

In 2010, I initiated a substantial research project to investigate how two different groups of stakeholders – teachers in schools (the curriculum implementers) and those appointed to support teachers' work (the curriculum advisers) – were coming to terms with the innovative requirements of the revised curriculum, seen from a task-based perspective. For me as a teacher educator, the project was significant. It enabled me to gain direct understanding of how teachers and advisers were interpreting revised curriculum requirements, including their own understandings (and misunderstandings) about TBLT, at an early stage in the curriculum implementation. The findings of the project were released in book form (East, 2012).

The voices of advisers, as reported in East (2012), revealed teacher uncertainty about enacting TBLT due to prior experiences with teacher-centred 'book-based learning' (p. 196), and highlighted 'a real need to actually promote task-based learning a lot more' (p. 195). With regard to teacher education initiatives, I recognised the need not only 'to explain and explore what TBLT means, including its theoretical rationales', but also 'to work with teachers in schools to help them to implement tasks' (p. 207) – that is, to hold theory and practice together in a critically reflective way. I recognised that my work as a teacher educator needed to be shaped by these core principles.

3.1.2 Changes to the Teaching Languages Course

From 2012, *Teaching Languages* underwent significant content renewal to reflect both revised curriculum aims and TBLT. East (2012) became the required text, due to its extensive context-embedded exploration of TBLT. The challenge became to support course participants as they transitioned into a new approach to L2 pedagogy. Programme participants came with a range of experiences of learning a language, and consequently beliefs about effective L2 teaching and learning. For many students, the language learning experiences that they went through when they were at school would likely have been teacher-dominated and grammar-based (this was certainly the most probable scenario for those who had undertaken their schooling in New Zealand). It was anticipated that these experiences would continue to exert an influence on thinking and understanding.

3.1.3 Supporting Reflection For-In-On Action

As a component of mediating curricular reform, the NZC proposes for teachers a cycle of classroom-centred reflective practice that provides an important vehicle for the exploration of innovation – a cycle known as *teaching as inquiry*. Building on the argument that 'effective pedagogy *requires* that teachers inquire into the impact of their teaching on their students' (Ministry of Education, 2007, p. 35, my emphasis), teaching as inquiry puts the teacher into the position of 'action researcher' in the context of undertaking a particular teaching sequence, and there is strong encouragement for teachers to utilise the teaching as inquiry cycle presented in the NZC.

The cycle was initially devised in the New Zealand context by Aitken and Sinnema (2008). The aim of the sequence is to help teachers find answers to the fundamental question 'what teaching approaches enhance outcomes for diverse learners?' The inquiry model has three elements, broadly parallel to reflection for-in-on action:

1. The initial *focusing inquiry* (a kind of reflection-for-action) is the space in which teachers identify a particular question to which they wish to pay attention. This might be an issue emerging in light of theory and the findings of prior research. It is anticipated that teachers will make decisions about what is important for their own students with regard to their current learning, and will establish appropriate learning goals. The focusing inquiry provides opportunities for teachers to consider innovative practices and plan for their implementation in a real classroom.

2. The *teaching inquiry* (a kind of reflection-in-action) is the space in which the teacher investigates the issue at hand. Teachers might draw on prior evidence from other contexts (e.g., theoretical frameworks; examples of effective practice) to plan and execute a teaching and learning sequence. With regard to innovation, the teaching inquiry (which would likely be implemented over a series of lessons or weeks) enables the collection of evidence about how the innovation is working in practice.

3. The *learning inquiry* (a kind of reflection-on-action) is the space in which teachers draw conclusions from their findings. Teachers are encouraged to look at students' learning outcomes, and then consider next steps for students' future learning. The learning inquiry provides teachers with post hoc opportunities to consider, based on evidence, whether and to what extent an innovation has worked. It also enables opportunities to consider how the teacher's practices should be adapted or amended in a future teaching as inquiry cycle. It is thus anticipated that one inquiry will lead to another.

The cycle supports the collection of evidence of classroom learning 'underpinned by a set of attitudes towards teaching and learning' (Aitken & Sinnema, 2008, p. 54). Three central attitudes support the model:

1. Open-mindedness – denotes 'a willingness to consider teaching approaches that may be unfamiliar or that may challenge one's beliefs about the best ways to teach', and openness to 'what the evidence shows about the effects of teaching on student learning' (p. 54). Open-mindedness with regard to innovation means being open to consider new approaches, especially those that conflict with prior beliefs.

2. Fallibility – recognises the context-bound nature of learning outcomes, and that different groups of learners may respond differently to a specific pedagogical approach or intervention. Fallibility with regard to innovation may

mean recognising that, just because an innovative approach appears not to have worked too well with one group of students, it may well work more positively with another group.

3. Persistence – represents a teacher's willingness to continue to inquire into their own practices as part of an ongoing cycle of reflection. Persistence with regard to innovation may mean persevering in the face of an apparent failure with an attempt to innovate.

The intersecting teaching as inquiry and reflection for-in-on action cycles became central to the interweaving of campus-based (theoretical under-standing) work and school-based (practical application) work in the LTE course. The cycles were supported by me in a range of ways. In what follows, I outline how the cycles, as illustrated in Figure 1, were facilitated in particular in Semester 1, where the primary focus was on pedagogical approaches (see also East, 2022).

The initial (on campus) block of time in Weeks 1–4 followed the pattern below:

1. A crucial starting point when it comes to preparing teachers to implement innovation is 'to make teachers more consciously aware of the beliefs about effective pedagogy that they currently hold, and the possible reasons for those beliefs' (East, 2022, p. 448). This establishes a baseline of beliefs. In Week 1 of the course, and as an opening activity (and also an opportunity for course participants to get to know one another), I asked participants to consider a range of statements about language teaching and learning and to indicate their strength of agreement with each statement. These statements were taken from Lightbown and Spada (2006, pp. xvii–xviii). This activity was undertaken individually at first, and then course participants shared their own perspectives with a partner.

2. After this initial individual and pair work, and still in Week 1, we engaged in a whole-group discussion. We looked in particular at statements that had generated a range of views. An important element of this activity was to make it clear to participants that beliefs are neither right nor wrong. This facilitated the creation of 'a safe environment in which these beginning teachers could think about and aim to identify their own beliefs, enter into discussion about how these beliefs might differ across individuals, and consider possible reasons for that' (East, 2022, p. 449).

3. Building on what had come out of these discussions, over Weeks 2 to 4 I took participants through a brief overview of the history of language teaching and learning and its expression in diverse approaches and methods. The purpose of this was to help participants to identify the potential root causes of their

current beliefs (i.e., links between their own beliefs and their prior learning experiences). This initial historical overview culminated in an introduction to TBLT and the central construct of task.

The first four weeks were designed to explore and challenge prior beliefs and assumptions about effective L2 pedagogy. They were also designed to set the beginning teachers up with a sufficient theoretical introduction to TBLT that could inform a particular inquiry that they would identify during their first school placement (*the focusing inquiry*). A good deal of the input at this stage was necessarily theoretical and methodological because it was anticipated that the practical applications would be covered by course tutors in the corequisite language-specific courses, as well as by the supervising mentor teachers in schools (known as Associate Teachers or ATs). Course delivery comprised lectures and readings in which key ideas and concepts were introduced to students. Video clips of teachers working in real classrooms, alongside small group and whole class discussion, were intended to help participants to unpack, reflect on and critique the input. During these weeks, my own reflections in and on action enabled me to guide and facilitate the discussions in ways that held in balance the theoretical/methodological perspectives being presented to the participants and their responses to these.

In Week 5, course participants had the opportunity, as part of their initial seven-week school placement, to spend the first week in their practicum school, principally to learn about the school and to observe some lessons. As part of this, I asked participants to note down their impressions of the extent to which any L2 lessons they observed fitted with the theories of language acquisition and language teaching methodologies that we had discussed during Weeks 1 to 4. The purpose of this was to help participants to map the ideas we had discussed onto the actual practices they observed.

Back on campus in Week 6, we worked as a whole group to unpack and discuss what had been observed. Once more, observed instances of practice were linked back through facilitated discussion to the theoretical ideas we had discussed prior to the observation. Week 7 provided the opportunity for participants to prepare for their own small-scale inquiries which were a major component of the partici-pants' official assignments for the course. The main portion of the first practicum placement (Weeks 8–13) provided the opportunity for the beginning teachers to set up a theoretically informed task-based inquiry (*the teaching inquiry*). There was a simple focus – at a minimum, participants were asked to draw on TBLT theory to design and implement at least one task with at least one class.

The final few weeks back on campus provided the opportunity for the beginning teachers to reflect on what had happened and to consider next steps.

In Week 14, we discussed and unpacked issues emerging from the beginning teachers' classroom experiences. In Week 15, they presented the outcomes of their teaching inquiries to their peers (*the learning inquiry*) as an assessed individual ten-minute presentation to the whole group. Participants were required to:

i. introduce the context (school type; class; language) and the task;
ii. justify the task as a task with reference to relevant literature;
iii. explain how its execution went and consider what changes might need to be made if the task were to be used again.

The essential purpose of this presentation assignment was to ensure evidence of critical reflection on the *practice* of TBLT in light of *theory*. In East (2022), I explained the core elements of the reflection:

> The teachers were encouraged to ask several key reflective questions: if something worked, what made it work? If something did not work, why didn't it work? What could have been done differently? What does this mean for theory? It was made clear to the students that, even if the task had not worked very well in their perception, this was a learning opportunity for them. Lack of success on one occasion provided opportunities to consider trying things out in a different way and evaluating how that might go. (p. 455)

Semester 2 (Weeks 16–30) followed a similar pattern. However, since in Semester 2 the focus was on language assessment, a parallel presentation assignment in the second half of the year focused on implementing and reflecting on an assessment opportunity, including (but not necessarily restricted to) using a communicative task for assessment purposes.

A second major coursework assignment (completing a reading log) was implemented across the whole year. At different points throughout the year, participants were required to read a chapter or chapters from East (2012) as the prescribed text, to think critically about the reading, and to reflect on its implications for practice. This year-long assignment was designed to be integrated with participants' school placements to facilitate the for-in-on action reflective cycles in Semesters 1 and 2 and to underpin the two teaching as inquiry cycles. In particular, the first reading log (completed a few weeks into the course, and before the participants had undergone any teaching practice in schools), and the last reading log (completed a few weeks before the end of the course, and after the participants had completed the two seven-week school placements in two different schools), contained a comparative (before-and-after) element. The essential purpose of this assignment was to ensure critical engagement with the *theory* about TBLT as well as critical reflection on its implications for *practice*.

4 A Longitudinal Research Project into Mediating Pedagogical Innovation

A critical issue for me as a teacher educator and researcher was the extent to which the input and assignments in the year-long *Teaching Languages* course enabled and enhanced change and development (i.e., an embracing and enacting of innovation). The two assignments I presented in Section 3.1.3 were designed to promote course participants' critical reflection for-in-on action in the context of their engagement with innovative ideas and as they inquired into their own practices. These assignments therefore provided primary data on potential shifts in thinking and practice among the participants.

The initial purpose of collecting the primary data was to document the beginning teachers' stories. However, as I began to analyse the first set of data (collected in 2012), I became very conscious that the findings were also raising questions and implications for my own practices as a language teacher educator. This prompted me to collect further data during the following years, primarily (and deliberately) from among the same set of participants at different times, and this time drawing on semi-structured interviews. Thus, over time, a cumulative picture was emerging of how beginning teachers grappled with and persevered with innovative ideas in the face of contextual realities.

A range of publications presents the *beginning teachers'* evolving professional practices and the issues these raised for *them* (East, 2014, 2017a, 2019a, 2019b, 2021b). In what follows, I use the teacher stories to describe how innovation was received by them. More importantly, I take a deliberate step back from the documented experiences of the teachers themselves, and bring the spotlight on to *me* as the teacher educator charged with encouraging innovation in the context of curricular reform. I reflect on and describe how teacher participants' reception of innovation informed and shaped my own beliefs and practices as an ITE teacher educator.

My data sources include 'text as the central prompt for the self-study process' (Tidwell et al., 2009, p. xiv). The primary texts in question were students' written coursework submissions and transcripts of interviews with subsets of participants, all of which were drawn on with appropriate ethical approval and the informed consent of the participants themselves. Secondarily, comments from several students' anonymous summative course evaluations were used as additional prompts for my own retrospective reflections. I draw extensively on the previously published accounts of the teachers' stories. I do this for several reasons – they: represent the outcomes of both cumulative and comparative data analysis; provide suitable but also succinct sources of open-ended feedback comments; have been subject to peer review which acted as a kind of 'critical friend' feedback on my interpretations of what was emerging. By way of exemplifying in this Element the full sets of data that were available to me, I also present, as individual vignettes, aspects of the raw data I collected at different points from the teacher participants. Each vignette focuses on data from one individual, taken from either a final reading log entry or an interview (pseudonyms are used). To make the vignettes succinct, individual comments from different points in the data sources are presented here as a single narrative, and transcript data were cleaned to support the readability of the narratives.

4.1 The First Study (2012)

As I explained in Section 3.1.2, 2012 was the first year in which significant shifts in the *Teaching Languages* course had occurred. I was interested in collecting data on how that had gone. The first investigation was framed as a non-experimental before-and-after study that compared participants' initial thinking, as evidenced in their first reading log entry, with summative thinking, as evidenced in their final log. Using a thematic analysis approach (Braun & Clarke, 2006), discrete characteristics (perceived advantages and drawbacks of TBLT) provided the primary units of analysis. The study was reported in East (2014).

In summary, an optimistic finding that was evident in the data was that confronting and developing beginning teachers' thinking and understandings through the interweaving of theory with practice had had positive impact on several participants' perspectives on TBLT as innovation (East, 2014, p. 269). For example, a position reported by one participant (Claire) was of being 'fairly doubtful about the effectiveness of TBLT at the beginning of the course'. However, actual task use was perceived as leading to 'very effective learning experiences' (Sharon) which were seen as 'beneficial to students' in terms of both 'mastery of the language and . . . motivation and engagement' (Faye).

Nevertheless, it became evident that contextual challenges were dampening some participants' enthusiasm. Several participants were circumspect with regard to future practices. TBLT could not be relied on as 'the sole approach' (Chen: East, 2014, p. 270), highlighting a need to 'experiment with different theories and approaches depending on our learners' (Sophia, p. 270). It seemed that, in part, teachers' circumspection was influenced by attitudes and under-standings held by more senior colleagues in the schools in which these teachers were working, including the mentor teachers to whom the students on practicum were attached (the ATs). This led one participant to conclude at the end of the programme that 'the main obstacle to TBLT' was 'the teachers themselves' (Frédéric, p. 271).

What I consider to be one of the biggest advantages of TBLT is the authenticity and real-life application of the tasks. Activities that are truly task-like will both engage the students and relate to their own lives. This makes it far more likely that the students will be interested and motivated to learn. . . . [But] there are still many things that confuse and maybe even concern me regarding the consideration of TBLT as not only the best, but the only way to teach in foreign language classrooms in New Zealand. . . . I think I would struggle to stick to a strong TBLT approach without stressing about whether my students are learning everything they need to.

In my personal opinion, it seems that many of the concerns raised about TBLT come from teachers who are perhaps less confident in their ability to effectively implement TBLT into their classroom, or who have had less exposure to it. . . . It is hard for me to envision a classroom environment that relies solely on TBLT as I had limited exposure to it throughout both my practicums. . . . Although my exposure to TBLT was rather limited on both practicums, I have found it useful to compare what I saw happening to what I can imagine would be happening if the teacher was using the TBLT approach.

When we first started learning about TBLT, I constantly compared it to my experience as a language learner, and how I had been taught. Now, however, I tend to think about what I have experienced myself, through teaching and learning. . . . The ideas presented throughout this course [*Teaching Languages*] and this book [East, 2012] have changed my outlook on teaching a language immensely. Before it started, I really had no idea what teaching a foreign language entailed, except what I could remember from being a language student myself. Throughout this year, I have been able to look back upon my experiences as a high school Spanish student and understand exactly what my teachers were doing and why they were doing it. At the time, I just took everything in and did my best to learn Spanish. Now, I have gained considerable knowledge of the theories that they were obviously employing in their teaching practices. I am excited to see what the future will bring and how I will manage to incorporate TBLT, and/or any other theories, into my classroom. It is all very well for me, now, to say that I will follow what the curriculum asks for and have a predominantly TBLT classroom environment, but in reality – who knows what will happen? I still believe that, in any class for any curriculum subject, the way you teach depends entirely on the requirements of the students. Once I know who I am teaching and in what context and which school, *then* I will be able to say how I will teach them.

4.2 Impacts on My Own Practices (2013–2014)

As I reflected on the evidence emerging from the initial study, a clash was apparent between the theory and emphases I was exploring with my students and the contextual realities these students were encountering in the field – the initial impact of the phenomenon of innovative ideas being 'washed out' (Zeichner & Tabachnick, 1981) as a consequence of occupational socialisation (Brouwer & Korthagen, 2005). This would inevitably be more problematic when the more dubious senior colleague was also the mentor AT. In other words, despite openness to innovation, tradition, it seems, was exerting a strong pull. Although this finding should not necessarily have been unanticipated, I was nevertheless taken somewhat by surprise. It seemed that the expectations of the revised curriculum (which had been around for several years by this stage and had been scaffolded in its introduction) were not filtering down sufficiently to some colleagues in some schools (see also Hipkins, 2010, in this regard). This meant that these beginning teachers were having to navigate a range of perspectives from more experienced colleagues in schools and were not necessarily seeing tasks in operation in classrooms.

In the process of reflection for future action, I made several changes to my practice. These changes required what I saw as the negotiation of a tricky path – one that, on the one hand, challenged the teachers to take a stance that was willing to try out an innovation in light of curricular reform, and, on the other hand, acknowledged the reality (and range) of debates about best practice that they would encounter both in the literature and in actual practice.

In the context of introducing and discussing the *theoretical underpinnings* of TBLT I made a number of adjustments:

1. I provided greater assurance that TBLT was developmentally an *extension* to earlier communicative practices, not an extreme and wholesale *overthrowing* of earlier practices, and that TBLT could live comfortably alongside more traditional elements. In this way, I was attempting to mitigate the claim or perception that TBLT was radically oppositional to existing practice, which had appeared, in some cases, to create barriers to considering it as a possible pedagogical approach.

2. I heightened participants' awareness that, when in schools, they would encounter a range of perspectives on TBLT among more senior colleagues. In this way, I was attempting to mitigate the arguments of more senior colleagues that TBLT should be rejected.

3. I stressed that it was important that these beginning teachers should be willing nonetheless to experiment with tasks, at least on one occasion and

at least with one class, and thereby see for themselves what happened. In this way, I was aiming to encourage teachers' continued engagement with innovative ideas.

It was also important for the teachers to take greater ownership of what *they* understood as a task for the purposes of TBLT. That is, in the first iteration of the course (2012), the tasks I introduced were theoretical (at least to the participants) in that they were examples generated from others, and not from them. I strengthened activities that aimed to replicate the core characteristics of a learner-centred task and embed participants' understandings of tasks more deeply into their thinking. At my disposal were the tasks that students in the 2012 cohort had developed and evaluated as part of their presentation assignment (e.g., see East, 2018). These were used to introduce subsequent student cohorts to actual (although not necessarily flawless) examples of tasks in action that their peers had come up with. I invited participants to think about, and come to their own conclusions on, the task-likeness of these tasks.

In one important task-based activity that followed on from the exploration of some of the 2012 cohort tasks, I set up six workstations, each representing one task type (Willis, 1996). Participants, in small groups, began at a designated station and wrote down on butcher paper an example of a task that fitted the type. After a few minutes, all groups rotated to a new station and added a further example to what became an expanding list until, at the conclusion, they arrived back at their original station and reviewed the whole list that had been created. The completed lists were subsequently written up to become a *participant-generated* taxonomy of task types, with examples, which the participants were able to take with them into their first practicum placement.

In several ways, therefore, I sought to moderate the negative effects of occupational socialisation by promoting a *continually* critically reflective stance that nonetheless acknowledged the limitations of contextual constraints. However, the limiting impact of occupational socialisation began to intrigue me. Brouwer and Korthagen (2005) suggested that 'the attitude development of prospective and beginning teachers' follows a U-shaped trajectory. That is, 'certain innovative attitudes are strengthened during preservice teacher education but are weakened again as graduates enter in-service teaching' (p. 156). Furthermore, Kosnik and Beck (2009) argued that research into teacher education programmes is limited when that research ends when the programme ends, thereby curtailing our ability to see the long-term professional growth potential of the programmes. I wanted to find out what actually happened over time to the teachers who had been part of the original 2012 cohort. I undertook a follow-up study in 2015.

4.3 The Second Study (2015)

The 2015 study (reported in East, 2019b) tracked a subset of the 2012 graduates after they had completed three years of work in schools ($n = 7$). I believed that this follow-up study was important in view of these teachers' pre-service experiences with more experienced colleagues. During their temporary school placements as student teachers, they were arguably in an unequal relationship with the more experienced teachers they were working alongside (and therefore arguably in a position of acquiescence to these colleagues' viewpoints). A key issue was the extent to which the innovative ideas presented in the ITE pro-gramme could be maintained three years after graduation, once these teachers had had opportunities to establish themselves, grown more comfortably into their profession, and, theoretically at least, moved to positions of greater equality with their peers. The findings here would help to determine the medium-term effectiveness of the original ITE exploration of innovation and might potentially raise issues that could shape further adjustments that might be required in the ITE course.

In the 2015 study, individual semi-structured interviews were used to uncover the extent to which, three years on, these ITE graduates continued to understand and enact task-based principles in their classrooms and continued to perceive barriers to successful implementation. Interviews were digitally recorded and transcribed. Emerging themes were highlighted and collated. Participants were subsequently invited to provide feedback on the interpretations and the extent to which these represented accurate reflections of their beliefs, thinking and experiences.

On the positive side, it seemed that participants had maintained their under-standing of key task characteristics as encountered during their ITE programme, and that they were, to a greater or lesser extent, attempting to put tasks into practice in their classrooms. There was also evidence that the ITE programme had been instrumental in helping these teachers to confront prior beliefs based on earlier experiences. Faye, for example, drew on words very reminiscent of an earlier (2012) reflection when she reported that she had appreciated the ITE focus on TBLT because it 'challenged my thoughts about language teaching'. It 'really helped me to think about what my beliefs were in language teaching and think about something new and different … right from the beginning of the year' (East, 2019b, p. 109).

Nevertheless, the real worlds of real classrooms continued to force these teachers to confront several constraints in practice. Among these were lack of ready-made resources and lack of time to create tasks. A broader culture of teacher-led pedagogy also continued to be seen as a hindrance. That is, as these newer colleagues worked alongside other colleagues, albeit in a more equal collegial role, they continued to be confronted with counter-attitudes that made introducing TBLT as innovation problematic. The confrontation was arguably starker than it had been when the beginning teachers had been on the ITE programme because now these teachers were working full-time in a school and were no longer temporary visitors who could return to the 'safety' of the university campus at the end of seven weeks. There was continued circumspection regarding TBLT in practice, this time arising from unfolding engagement with classroom realities.

VIGNETTE 2: FRANK – INTERVIEW AFTER THREE YEARS OF TEACHING
(SEE ALSO EAST, 2017A, 2019B)

I came away [from the 2012 course] with a very clear understanding of what constituted a task, you know, the criteria over task, what were the theoretical underpinnings of those principles, how that integrated into . . . the New Zealand curriculum in terms of communication being core . . . I do like TBLT in its general approach towards language acquisition and the experiential and the authentic nature of it, which fundamentally is what learning a language should be about, right? . . . So TBLT is great for taking authentic materials and bringing them into a classroom to deliver what we can of an authentic experience without actually going to that place. Much, much more authentic than a textbook or 'I'm going to tell you about this grammar thing', 'memorise your vocab' kind of stuff. And it's experiential in the sense that the kids are doing it, it's led by them, but guided by you. So once the resources are created, it's very hands off, you know, the kids are doing it themselves with you there to steer them . . .

[But there is a] dichotomy between learning about it on paper and going 'this is TBLT', and then just dipping our toes into it on practicum, and then taking that knowledge and delivering it as part of a syllabus where we are teaching five or six classes . . . That is why a book or a bunch of resources that are pre-prepared and ready to just be delivered or adapted to be delivered in a school would be super useful for me, because it's not for lack of wanting to, it is just a practical restraint on time. . . . The lack of go to resources for task-based is a problem. . . . [Also] TBLT is not well picked up inside the teaching community . . . some of us would go into classrooms and we wouldn't be allowed to teach in a task-based approach. . . . It is actually the kids as well. They don't always want to do a TBLT style or task-like approach . . . some kids want the upfront grammar, and if . . . they are saying 'we want that', who am I to say no to them, you know?

The training at teachers' college was helpful . . . it is actually important that that message [about innovation] goes out there . . . [because] a huge chunk of the teaching profession . . . were taught differently. They have a different idea of what language teaching is that they brought with them from 30 or 40 years' experience and their training programmes. And we are trying to implement something new. So that's going to take a long time. I mean a long, long, long time. And it is going to require consistency of the training programmes too over a long period of time . . . it's a significant investment of time and energy to make [innovation] happen . . .

I think that the best that one can expect from a teacher training programme is to deliver what research and experience and so forth demonstrate through evidence as best practice and as most beneficial in terms of reaching the stated goals of the curriculum, be those learning objectives or the overall underpinnings of communication. . . . What is the alternative? Not delivering at all and having zero informing of teaching practice with TBLT being sort of integrated into it, you know? I think not delivering best practice as part of a teacher training programme would be remiss. . . . [but] the particular pedagogy that a teacher takes forward into their own classroom is up to them. . . . Ultimately, you have to look at your kids and you go 'what is going to lead to the best learning outcome for you?' I remember reflecting at the time [of my ITE] and saying it wouldn't be the sole approach that I would take . . . However, the theoretical underpinnings of TBLT, which also underpin other communicative pedagogies . . . those things play out in my classroom in whatever approach I'm taking . . .

4.4 Impacts on My Own Practices (2015–2016)

Several positive and assuring findings emerged from the interview data collected towards the end of 2015 (and analysed in the course of 2016). Although it was apparent that the ITE programme was limited (i.e., it could only ever enable participants to take small, initial steps), theoretical understandings around tasks did appear to persist after three years, and attempts were made to continue to use tasks. There was also, it seemed, clear perceived value in exploring the innovation with beginning teachers. The study also reconfirmed the constraints to innovation that had emerged in the original 2012 study. Two clear messages stood out:

1. Teachers needed clear examples of tasks in practice
2. Teachers would still resort to a range of practices.

These messages reinforced the changes to course delivery I had begun to make, and indicated that the course was probably going in an appropriate direction. Thus, as I began to move into 2017, two new questions intrigued me as a teacher educator as I sought to reflect on and learn from the cumulative evidence I was gathering.

First, since the 2012 cohort was the first to have undergone the course with a dedicated focus on TBLT, the data I collected were what I described at the time as 'a preliminary evaluation of the effectiveness of the programme in developing participants' understandings of TBLT' (East, 2014, p. 264). The data indicated what emerged at that time as 'a genuine tension between encouraging TBLT as innovation (through teacher education) and moderating TBLT in practice in the light of genuine constraints' (p. 272). With regard to my own practices as a language teacher educator, I had made some modifications as a consequence of the successes and challenges emerging, and I had begun to draw some conclusions about effective teacher education with regard to encouraging innovation. Especially in view of the changes I had implemented, I wanted to re-evaluate the effectiveness of the ITE programme, essentially addressing the question of whether modifications to my own practices actually made a difference. In 2017, I replicated the 2012 study.

Second, the follow-up study I instigated in 2015 provided some evidence of the sustainability of innovative practices in light of ITE experiences, but did not consider the place of PLD in consolidating knowledge and understanding. My findings therefore did not enable me to draw any conclusions about the impact that PLD initiatives for in-service teachers might make, whereas such PLD is one means through which teachers can be supported to take further steps and to continue to grow in their practice. I wanted to find out more about the potential impact of PLD and what that might reveal about ITE practices. In 2017, I carried out a new study that took PLD into account.

4.5 The Third Study (2017)

The study that I undertook with the 2017 beginning teacher cohort (reported in East, 2021b) was framed as a 'purposeful replication' (Norris & Ortega, 2006, p. 8), designed to provide space for me to *reconsider* what I had uncovered in the original 2012 study in a new and more informed light (Porte, 2013; Porte & McManus, 2019). To that end, it drew on the same data collection methods as the original study.

Evidence from the 2017 cohort suggested that there were theory and practice informed shifts in thinking and understanding among participants with regard to the value of TBLT as innovation. The perspectives of two teachers of Chinese (both L1 speakers of Mandarin) bring this out.

Feng noted that before she had begun to engage with TBLT ideas, her perceptions of 'a good teacher and a good teaching practice' had tended to be 'a traditional PPP model where the teacher has to know everything (almost everything) and be the authority of the knowledge delivered in the classroom' (East, 2021b, p. 560). A shift in perspective enabled Feng to see that TBLT offered a contrasting approach that enhanced authentic language use in class and provided opportunities for learner interaction in the L2. These perspectives mirrored the shifts in practice identified by Brown (2014) that I outlined at the start of this Element. Feng concluded that this kind of pedagogical approach should become central to all L2 teaching.

Chun declared that her last engagement with L2 learning had been in school, almost twenty years prior to joining the ITE programme. Her assumption at the start of the course had been that there would still be an emphasis on the basics of vocabulary and grammar. The promotion of TBLT, which she described as 'an innovative teaching method towards language teaching', had surprised her. Her initial attempts to consider TBLT generated some stress as she attempted to 'overwrite the system in my head' because 'you want to cling onto something that you are comfortable and familiar with' (East, 2021b, p. 561). Nonetheless, by the time of writing her final reading log, she asserted:

> But the more I learn about TBLT, the more I try to implement it, the more I am fascinated by it. When I see students actively communicate with each other in class, I think – this is going to be the way. When I see students fighting hard to achieve their goals for the task using the target language, I think – this is the way. When students ask me 'Miss, what are we going to do tomorrow? Can we do some more of those tasks?' I think this has to be the way.
>
> (East, 2021b, p. 561)

Despite these positive assertions of substantial growth and development and an apparent positive embracing of innovation (both of which could also be traced in the data available from the 2012 cohort), there was also (as with the 2012 cohort) a level of circumspection among some participants. As Serafina expressed it, 'at the end, it is the job of the teacher to find the right balance of approaches that fit their students' abilities and learning styles'. Chun concluded, 'is TBLT our final answer for language teaching? The answer is probably no' (East, 2021b, p. 562).

A crucial issue for me was whether modifications I had made to my own practices (see Section 4.2) would have an influence on 2017 participants' thinking and understanding about TBLT in comparison with the 2012 group. I concluded that the comparative reproduction provided 'accumulative evidence that, at least between the two points of evaluation (2012 and 2017), the course was continuing to fulfil its primary function, and suggests ongoing appreciation among participants of the principles and benefits of TBLT' (East, 2021b, p. 562).

As I wrestled with the concern that perhaps I had watered TBLT down too much in my accommodation to teachers' reticence (whether the reservations of beginning teachers or the resistance of more senior colleagues), it seemed that I had still managed to highlight TBLT as innovation in ways with which these beginning teachers were able to identify. The continued acceptance of a range of practices and approaches in the L2 classroom was not unanticipated, given the accommodations I had made and the realities of classroom contexts. Curiously, a quantitative statistical comparison of frequency of comments (both advantages and drawbacks of TBLT) demonstrated no statistically significant differences between the two cohorts (see East, 2021b, p. 558). This comparison must of course be interpreted in light of the very small sample sizes and the principally qualitative nature of the data. Nonetheless, the modifications I had made to my own practices did not appear to have made any substantial difference to course outcomes (I reflect on the implications of this in Section 5.4).

VIGNETTE 3: JANELLE — END-OF-YEAR READING LOG REFLECTIONS
(SEE ALSO EAST, 2021B)

I learned Japanese through a PPP model at school and university. I gained fluency through immersion while working in Japan. After university I taught EFL in the grammar-translation heavy context of Japan. I tried valiantly to make classes what I considered to be more 'communicative', through introduction of role-plays or speaking/writing free production opportunities for students. Though I found this sometimes worked, it often failed. Partly due to my own lack of training. In the end I found myself adapting my activities to suit the test-focused grammar-translation model of the context I was in. . . . I arrived at teacher education on the back of this experience, frustrated that I hadn't been able to introduce my students to real language or have them be able to use it and disappointed in my own shortcomings in EFL teaching. Here I was introduced to TBLT . . . [and] initially it was a lot to take in. With the explanation of theory and logic behind TBLT I was in principle on board with it and considered it to potentially be a powerful, game-changing tool in instructed language acquisition, but was still confused how to actually implement it. . . . It seemed daunting and scary, even if I understood some of the theoretical underpinnings.

Based on my experience during practicums one and two I now see TBLT as achievable for teachers and more importantly engaging, fun and beneficial for students. . . . I was able to see it in action at first practicum, even if I wasn't fully aware of it at the time. . . . [I] saw just how much fun the students at practicum one had been having while using the language through TBLT. In contrast [in] my practicum two class . . . the students didn't seem to be having that same experience, enjoying playing with and trying out language. The classes were predominately teacher-led and explanation heavy. . . . The stark contrast between the two teaching styles in practicum highlighted and reinforced for me what I had already conceptualised in my head but was yet to see in practice, that TBLT was a powerful tool for enjoyable, memorable and effective language teaching. To see first-hand the difference it made in classrooms was heartening and has left me feeling empowered going into my first year of teaching.

I think old habits do die hard. . . . At the end of the day, I think it is most important that students enjoy the experience of learning a new language. One shouldn't be dogmatic in one's beliefs in a certain way of teaching and learning. In light of this course I have come to see that there is no single best way of teaching a language, it is important to consider multiple ways of doing things and selecting from a repertoire of teaching styles depending on our context, our learners, our schools and goals. Research, expectations of schools and what is considered best practice are always changing, much like languages themselves do. To ignore these changes or to disavow them is not only futile but will also result in us seeming outdated or archaic.

4.6 The Fourth Study (2017)

Reflecting on the comparative findings (2012 and 2017), I issued an important caveat in East (2021b). My findings from both the studies had revealed that, despite a revised curriculum that was guiding the work of all colleagues in schools, currently serving teachers could be a particular hindrance to innovation –

a concern that Frédéric had neatly encapsulated (see Section 4.1). Also, teachers do not suddenly 'arrive' as a consequence of completing an ITE qualification. Rather, there is the potential for continual growth and development as teachers not only become more secure in their own teaching, but also engage, in a much more direct way, with the persistent day-to-day realities of real classrooms.

In 2017, and at the same time as the replication study, I initiated a second follow-up study (reported in East, 2019a). Its purpose was to continue the tracking of 2012 graduates and to collect further data on the practising teacher variable. However, this time the study focused on just two of the participants after they had completed five years of work in schools – Stefano and Sancho, two teachers of Spanish. The selection criterion was that these two participants were the only two from the 2012 cohort to have taken part in the follow-up study in 2015 and *also* to have completed, in 2017, a dedicated one-year PLD programme, undertaken in the context of a full-time teaching position – the *Teacher Professional Development Languages* (TPDL) programme.

In the New Zealand context, the TPDL programme (introduced in 2005 and running until 2018) represented a significant PLD enterprise (see East, 2012, for an introduction, and Erlam & Tolosa, 2022, for an informative evaluation). As with the ITE course *Teaching Languages*, it had a strong focus on TBLT. A component was a credit-bearing course, *Teaching Languages in Schools*, which was in several respects a pared-down version of the ITE course, delivered in several two-day blocks throughout the year. A crucial element of the course was the use of an assessed small-scale teaching as inquiry project (see Section 3.1.3). Similarly to the ITE participants' presentation assignment, the project was designed to investigate the impact and effectiveness of using a communicative task with a participant's own class.

The follow-up study provided an important opportunity to consider longitudinal developments alongside a small-scale occasion to investigate the extent to which subsequent PLD helped to consolidate two early career teachers' experiences and success. Although I was not involved in the delivery of the PLD programme, my study represented a bridge between pre-service and in-service teacher education, and the prospect of considering the programme's impact in light of an ITE exposure to TBLT as innovation. My study sought to provide some evidence of the extent to which a supported *reinquiry* into these two teachers' own practices made any further impact on their continuing openness to and acceptance of TBLT as innovation. Data sources included the written projects that were presented for assessment purposes that outlined the outcomes of the teaching as inquiry process, and individual follow-up interviews after both participants had completed the programme. Once more, interviews were digitally recorded and transcribed. Emerging themes were highlighted and collated. The two participants were subsequently invited to provide feedback on the interpretations, and the extent to which these represented accurate reflections of their beliefs, thinking and experiences.

At the time of the PLD, Stefano was working in a school that he described as very traditional, and textbook- and examination-driven. He recognised that, since his ITE in 2012, his application of task-based ideas was becoming weaker as he increasingly adopted a teacher-led stance. In 2015, he had acknowledged his own eclecticism in practice as he grappled with classroom realities. Believing that the PLD programme might support him with reintroducing TBLT in a contextually appropriate way, Stefano set out to undertake an inquiry cycle to help him to 'prove it is possible to continue without following a traditional method ... prove that they can still learn Spanish by following a task-based approach' (East, 2019a, p. 148). The inquiry process enabled him to recognise afresh his role as a facilitator of his students' learning. When his students encountered problems as they undertook a task, he encouraged them to experiment and try to find their own solutions, something that he observed they could virtually always do. He acknowledged, however, that a tension remained, especially in the very traditional context in which he worked. He concluded with a comment reminiscent of his perspective in 2015 – 'I still think it is very difficult to teach task-based' (p. 151).

Sancho was working in a school that was arguably more conducive to a constructivist approach. Nevertheless, and in common with Stefano, an important shift that Sancho wished to make, and for which the PLD became a useful catalyst, was to move his practices somewhat away from teacher-led and for his students to undertake more work more autonomously. Sancho acknowledged that a dedicated focus on TBLT at the ITE level had been useful, but conceded that, in his experience, this had ended up being more theoretical than practical. Since, in his perception, TBLT was essentially an experiential innovation, the practical reality was that, instead, it was easier to opt for something that was more controlled, especially in the first few years of teaching. Now in his fifth year of teaching, and having become more relaxed and experienced, Sancho saw the timing of the PLD programme as ideal. He noted that the PLD programme did not actually introduce him to any concepts or ideas that he had not already encountered during his ITE back in 2012. Rather, the PLD was a means of consolidating ideas to which he was open but which had thus far remained largely abstract.

It was really useful [to do this in 2012] – [as a consequence] I knew the theory, and I think when we finish [the course at] university we all know the theory really well because that whole year is about that. But putting that into practice, that is the problem, you know, because ... [becoming a teacher] is a new start, a new thing, [and] ... you go for the easy thing and do it, and you tick all the boxes, and you go on holiday, and that's all you need. ... Especially the first and second year [of teaching], you just survive any way you can. Then I think my fourth and fifth year, I think it was I felt like I had more time to reflect on my practices and changing them. ... [It is] quite good to actually reflect on what we are doing and the way we are doing [it] and why we are doing it. So, I thought that [the PLD] was a great opportunity ... for me to actually think about my teaching ... I thought also the time was perfect – five years. I believe it is a good time because you can consolidate and you feel more comfortable with your teaching. ... I find that after so many years I am a little bit more relaxed with teaching – the first two years, as I say, you don't even have the time to think about things. ... I would say that [the PLD] has definitely improved [my practice] and made me reflect for different reasons ...

I don't think there has been a lot of new knowledge or new information, but it has been again consolidating what I knew, for me to internalise more on the benefits of task-based and improve ... Now I know the theory, and I know a little bit better how to apply [it] – the most important thing I know [now is] the importance of applying it. ... [Earlier on] I still thought it was important to stick with the programme and apply a pre-planned programme with content ... I think last year I already started applying or changing my methodology, [realising] that it is not that important to actually cover everything that you have in mind ... it is not about that quantity, but about the quality of the teaching and the learning, therefore, task-based gives the opportunity for the students to actually not go so fast, but actually understand better what they do ... I know that at the end of the year they will retain the knowledge that they gain from that time. ... they are speaking more Spanish in class, they are using more with more confidence ...

I think I am [now] more aware of the importance of task-based teaching ... One thing that I learned and ... am applying in a more deliberate way is for me to be less teacher-centred, for the students to do more work independently ... for me to organise the task in advance ...

and then for the students to take control of the task. I feel like before this year I had some activities that were tasks but still there was a lot of input before, during and after the task. Now there is a lot of work before, and then, during it, just checking what the students are doing, and it has worked better and is a more pleasant way of teaching. That is probably the main thing that I have changed in my practices . . .

The only thing I still think – [TBLT] was just one [way] . . . I think it is the way to go, don't get me wrong, it was fantastic and I think it is great, task-based for teaching languages . . . but I thought the whole year was just focused on . . . that one way of teaching . . . I would have preferred if there were some other ways, some other ideas, some other focus . . . exploring different approaches that have been proven . . . We know that the core of the curriculum is communication so it would be silly to approach grammar as a core of any programme, but just giving some ideas . . . hand in hand with task-based teaching.

4.7 Final Reflections (2017)

As I reflected on the stories emerging from these two teachers' experiences, I concluded that, for those who already brought with them a level of prior knowledge and understanding of task-based principles, one year of dedicated and inquiry-based PLD was 'a significant step in embedding these principles into teachers' on-going work' (East, 2019a, p. 156). Furthermore, returning to the U-shaped curve analogy drawn by Brouwer and Korthagen (2005), there was, in this very small-scale study, some evidence to suggest that innovative attitudes strengthened during ITE and weakened during early practice can be potentially restrengthened after a number of years, thereby reversing the U and perhaps beginning an upwards trajectory.

Brouwer and Korthagen (2005) noted that beginning teachers can face genuine struggles around control at the beginning and go through a process that is 'more one of survival than of learning from experiences'. Novice teachers, who may not have felt sufficiently prepared by their ITE, may have 'come to view colleagues in their schools as "realistic" role models, as the people who "do know" how one should go about teaching' (p. 155). These perspectives are reflected in the conflicting tensions described by both Sancho and Stefano. After the initial few years, learning from the actual experiences of real classrooms over which teachers can exercise control arguably provides a realistic environment to return to innovative ideas at a later stage, and to try them out again.

Despite the fact that both these teachers did not necessarily embrace the innovative ideas introduced to them in their ITE as wholeheartedly as I, as an ITE teacher educator, may have wished to see, it is clear that beliefs and thinking *were* challenged and disrupted at that early stage in these teachers' development, a finding that was also in evidence in the other studies I had undertaken. It is also clear that the ITE initiative enabled seeds of innovation to be sown, and these seeds could give rise to a subsequent seeking out of further opportunities to explore the innovation, and thereby to embed it somewhat more successfully into practice. It seems, then, that an ITE focus on innovation is important, but is just the beginning of a longer-term journey. This needs to be acknowledged as a backdrop to whatever innovations are promoted at the ITE level.

5 Discussion

The key purpose of this Element has been to document how I applied critical reflection to my own work as an ITE language teacher educator as I drew on evidence emerging from ITE participants over a number of years. The outcomes of this self-study have revealed several important considerations both for my own evolving practices and for effective teacher education.

Van den Branden's (2009a) claim that teachers teach in the way they themselves were taught and may be strongly resistant to change illustrates not only the pervasive influence of established beliefs shaped by early learning experiences but also the crucial need for teacher education initiatives that can challenge beliefs, thereby facilitating change (Borg, 2003, 2011; 2015; Cabaroglu & Roberts, 2000; Ha & Murray, 2021; Richards et al., 1996). This is particularly important where the emphasis is on innovating practice. Whatever the context, innovation challenges, questions and confronts more established ways of doing things.

As a way of mediating innovation, I proposed a cyclical model of reflection – reflection for-in-on action – that would enable a strong theory-practice connection to be established. The evidence from the studies I have presented is that, at the very least, one key outcome of the LTE in which I engaged with the teachers is that participants appear to have learned the importance of reflecting on their own practices. This is a crucial starting point for enhancing practice and initiating change.

In the course of applying the three-component cycle to my own work, I came to recognise two tensions which found expression in the data I collected (and which are exemplified in the vignettes I presented):

1. On the one hand, a focus on innovation can make positive differences to beliefs and practices, and this is a reassuring finding.

There was evidence that prior beliefs can be challenged and innovative practices can be embraced *and* sustained by beginning teachers (in this case, teachers saw value in using communicative language use tasks, and this perception of value was often maintained even after graduation from the programme). As one participant (Frank) said after three years of teaching in the classroom, 'I mean, let's be honest, if we weren't taught [about TBLT], we would all be standing up the front of the classroom doing the PPP. Ignorance is bliss, if we didn't know about it we wouldn't do it' (East, 2019b, p. 109). The implication here is that there is value in making innovations transparent. Both the status quo and a reliance on more traditional practices can be shifted, not necessarily radically, but certainly in the direction of the innovation.

2. On the other hand, teachers do not blindly and uncritically accept and adopt innovative practices. Rather, they make choices.

The choices teachers make might include several more traditional elements. Some of these choices may be contingent on external contextual factors such as other colleagues' attitudes and practices. They may also be contingent on responding to what is actually happening in the local classroom context (e.g., how the learners are receiving the innovation). As Frank also put it after three years of teaching, 'I currently use TBLT, I also use "chalk and talk", I also use silent reading, I use textbooks, I use the internet, you know – it is one of a suite of tools' (East, 2019b, p. 111). The implication here is that innovations will inevitably become part of a broader package that may well include more traditional components. This does not mean the push towards innovation has been unsuccessful.

There is a tension between the two classroom realities stated above. Griffiths (2012) noted that 'teachers are individuals with their own . . . individual differences, beliefs, and characteristics' (p. 475). Kayi-Aydar et al. (2019) expressed the tension that emerges like this – as teachers 'engage [on the one hand] in innovative teaching practices, adapt themselves to changing situations, [and on the other] meet expectations and requirements in their work environment and implement policies, they "exercise" agency to make choices and decisions' (p. 1). Kayi-Aydar et al.'s commentary reveals the potentially incompatible pressures with which teachers have to deal, which may set limits on the true exercise of teacher autonomy and teachers' ability to implement innovation. Teacher agency is therefore, in their words, 'shaped by a myriad of factors', which may well include 'dominant discourses, power and hierarchies, conflicts, tensions and dilemmas'. These factors may, on the one hand, 'prevent teachers from engaging in acts and actions that they desire', thereby limiting agency. They may, on the other hand, be factors that 'push teachers to engage in acts of resisting, challenging and criticizing, thereby promoting teacher agency'. This ultimately makes teacher agency 'unpredictable and contextually complex' (p. 1).

Also, teachers, it seems, make their own independent choices about enacting aspects of innovation as they respond to local realities. As Mitchell et al. (2019) expressed it, 'teachers "read" and interpret the changing dynamics of the learning context from moment to moment, and take what seem to *them* to be appropriate contingent actions, in the light of *largely implicit, automatized pedagogical knowledge'* (p. 406, my emphases). Thomas and Brereton (2019) observed that teachers often simply 'prefer to *get on with it'* (p. 276) and 'go with their own instincts regarding what works, what gets a good reaction, and what engages learners' (p. 278).

Depending on where teacher educators position themselves in the debates around effective L2 pedagogy and implementing innovation, teachers' classroom autonomy, including the potential to modify or reject innovation, may be viewed in one of two ways. It may be seen as a limiting factor (i.e., one that *enables* teachers to choose which elements of practice they will adopt or adapt, even when these elements of practice may seem, from the perspective of innovation, to be inappropriate or limiting). Alternatively, it may be seen as a wise consequence of critically reflective teacher education (i.e., one that *empowers* teachers to choose their practices freely, including incorporating aspects of tradition). (As Kayi-Aydar et al., 2019, intimated, this begs the question of how autonomous teachers actually are as they grapple with often competing contextual demands, but that question is beyond the scope of this Element.)

The two tensions I have summarised above – the apparent embracing of innovation alongside the inevitable accommodations to contextual realities, or, as I described it towards the start of this Element, the pull of tradition against the push of innovation – became the double-edged sword with which I had to contend as I reflected for-in-on my own actions as a teacher educator.

5.1 Implications for S-STEP

With regard to my own work and the longitudinal study I undertook between 2012 and 2017, I am mindful of Tidwell et al.'s (2009) argument that 'in the course of a given study, important and yet subtle aspects of the researcher's practice as a teacher educator may actually be transformed without conscious awareness, and such transformations may only come to be recognized through post hoc reflections' (p. xiv). In the course of the six years of work that I outlined in Section 4 of this Element, the application of the three-component cycle has meant that my own understandings about TBLT as innovation and its introduction in the instructed context were deepened, refined and honed. Furthermore, my practices as a teacher educator changed in subtle but important ways. Several changes were, however, *with* conscious awareness.

I began, in 2012, with a highly optimistic belief that, as a consequence of curricular reform, a new generation of language teachers would see the importance of innovation and could become catalysts for change in their subsequent work. The data I began to collect spoke to a different scenario with which I had to deal.

Bergmark et al. (2018) asserted, 'teacher education must reflect a *realistic* and not an *idealised* picture of the teaching profession' (p. 278, my emphases). As I undertook the process of 'listening to what our students have to say and observing carefully how they react to the practices we engage in with them' (Hamilton & Pinnegar, 2014, p. 145), my stance on innovation began to shift. This was done primarily as a means of preparing participants better for what I came to realise, quite early on, was the pervasive influence of the realities they would face in school classrooms.

The fact that teachers may continue to teach in largely teacher-fronted ways, even when confronted with innovative ideas, should perhaps not have surprised me. Brouwer and Korthagen (2005) spoke of 'a rift between idealistic notions developed during teacher education programs, on the one hand, and pressure from schools to rely on traditional patterns of behavior, on the other' (p. 155). My own initial idealistic notions of what might be possible became tempered by the contextual realities.

Furthermore, Hyland and Wong (2013) wrote that what is considered to be novel 'resides in *perception*; how something is *seen* by teachers ... or others involved in its implementation' (p. 2, my emphases). To accommodate the contextual realities more effectively, I made a number of adaptations to practice (see also Section 4.2):

- I provided greater room for participants to come to their own conclusions about what the innovation should look like in the language classroom (i.e., I encouraged participants' freedom to adapt tasks to their own developing understandings and contexts, which might mean using tasks in the broader setting of more traditional approaches or teacher-led moments). In this way, I sought to encourage a perception of TBLT that might be less 'threatening' – that is, not as something that is radically in opposition to more established practices, but as something that can be laid alongside these practices. After all, a perspective on implementing innovation that 'tends to take the shape of a revolution that turns the familiar world of the language classroom upside down ... is not how successful innovations in education are usually realized' (Van den Branden, 2022b, pp. 641–642).

- I strengthened opportunities for participants to come to their own hands-on (albeit theory informed) conclusions about what tasks were, so that the construct of task was more rooted into their thinking (i.e., my approach became more experiential).
- I continued to insist that these teachers needed to devise and implement a task with a real class, and continued to make this an assessed (and therefore perceptually important) element of the course (i.e., I was not letting these teachers off the hook with regard to experimenting with innovation, even though I was placing that experiment within an arguably more accommodating context). That is, 'taking local conditions into account . . . is not the same as conceding to them as determinants of what can be done. There must always be the possibility of change' (Widdowson, 1993, p. 271).

Against the foreground of subtle and yet deliberate changes to practice lies a background which Hamilton and Pinnegar (2014) acknowledged as an impetus for teacher educator reflection, a 'space in practice where a teacher educator experiences a living contradiction' (p. 148). In practice, I experienced a range of living contradictions (or tensions) that challenged my beliefs about pedagogical effective practice and the implementation of innovation. These tensions arose both from how the course and programme were structured and from wider considerations of what constitutes effective L2 pedagogy in instructed settings.

5.1.1 The Tension between Promoting Innovation and Teacher Autonomy

The acceptance of teacher autonomy, and especially the autonomy of the beginning or novice teacher to make choices that may run counter to what the teacher educator would ideally like to see, is an important lesson for teacher educators to learn. This reality is exemplified in the S-STEP literature. One language arts teacher educator noted a clash between her espoused commitment to a constructivist approach and her reactions to some of her students' expressed beliefs (Grierson, 2010, p. 7). Grierson was, for example, 'surprised when some shared beliefs that were incongruous with recommended approaches' and 'found it difficult to facilitate non-threatening discussions about their divergent perspectives', an experience she found 'disconcerting'. She recognised that it was nonetheless also important to 'create a "safe" environment for candidates to share their beliefs', making this navigation, in her view, 'akin to walking a slippery tightrope'. A crucial reflective question for her therefore became, 'if I am really a constructivist, why did I want my students to construct understandings that are in line with my conceptions of instruction?' For me, the idealism of 'changing the world' in light of curricular reform needed to become moderated. This was because I was committed to establishing a safe environment for the exploration of ideas and practice. This allowed for the emergence of inevitable questioning of the innovation at hand as the beginning teachers began to challenge some of its assumptions and outworkings.

5.1.2 The Tension between Sage on Stage and Guide on Side

In the ITE context I have described here, this was, at the end of the day, an academic programme, and a balance was required between theory and practice across all the courses participants were required to take. *Teaching Languages* inevitably had a strong theoretical/methodological element because it was anticipated that the practical and specialist (i.e., language-specific) input would largely be left up to individual tutors (in the language-specific courses) and mentor colleagues (in schools). With regard to the requirement to explore the *theoretical and methodological* dimensions of TBLT as innovation, I started my work in 2012 with the belief that these were better explained to students than discovered experientially. This replication of a more traditional top-down approach to knowledge dissemination raised several questions as I grappled with how my students were struggling with TBLT. In particular, I wanted to respond to early feedback, collected through summative evaluations, that indicated that teachers wanted more hands-on experience of working with tasks – more practice, less theory.

Certainly, the presentation and reading log assignments I have described passed ownership of knowledge discovery and reflection over to the beginning teachers themselves. However, when the perceived benefits of a social/experiential approach vis-à-vis a directly instructional model are open to critique (Coe et al., 2014; Kirschner et al., 2006), this raises the fundamental issue of *guide on the side* contrasted with *sage on the stage,* and how these two apparently opposing approaches to pedagogy are to be reconciled in the most effective ways. My early identified struggle between imparting theoretical knowledge to students (top-down) in contrast to letting students discover the theoretical knowledge for themselves (bottom-up) is, it seems, a concern experienced by others engaged in S-STEP research.

Building on the argument that many teacher educators have not received any specific prior instruction in the learner-centred approaches that they are encouraging pre-service teachers to adopt in their own classroom practices, one science teacher educator described his own experiences as a 'living contradiction' (Buttler, 2020). As he explained, 'I brought my [top-down] teaching approach to teacher education unchallenged and without reflection' (p. 233). This meant that, in practice, 'if I believed my students should shift their understandings, I used didactic strategies to enact change' (p. 235). Even so, Buttler believed that adequate and relevant teacher education requires participants to be 'exposed to a constructivist, student-centred teaching approach' (p. 235). He sought to shift his own practices accordingly.

Similarly to Buttler, I changed aspects of my practice to model a more constructivist approach (e.g., the hands-on participant-focused exploration of task types – see Section 4.2). Nonetheless, I maintained aspects of top-down delivery of theory, albeit a delivery that invited participant questioning and discussion and thereby brought the participants into the ideas being presented.

5.1.3 The Tension between Successfully Innovating and Stakeholder Buy-In

With regard to exploring the language-specific *practical outworkings* of TBLT, Long (2016) argued that the successful adoption of TBLT as innovation relies on expertise in TBLT among all stakeholders, alongside a considerable amount of time and effort invested in the innovation. Long did not underestimate the focused and supported attention that would be needed, and the requirement for all stakeholders to 'move forward together systematically in what must be a collaborative endeavor' (p. 29). Hyland and Wong (2013) suggested that it is 'futile, as many innovators have found, to change just one aspect of a national policy, institutional plan, classroom approach or beliefs of one group. Stakeholders need to "learn change" together' (p. 3). Optimum conditions require courses and programmes that can be largely illustrative of the innovation in question, supported by colleagues who believe in the innovation and who are themselves largely working in accordance with the innovation. Systemic barriers can mean in practice that 'many teachers who *do* engage in trying to innovate their classroom practice have the feeling that they are swimming against the tide' (Van den Branden, 2022a, p. 234).

In the case in question, initial efforts to promote TBLT were undermined when the tutors responsible for the language-specific courses in the programme did not understand or advocate the approach. This was a variable that was not easily controllable, and time and resources were not available to upskill or acclimatise them concerning the orientation of the programme. A significant structural change took place in 2013 when I invited a colleague (Constanza Tolosa) to take over a substantial generic component of the corequisite specialist languages courses. Constanza and I worked collaboratively to ensure complementarity between our courses, with my contribution focusing more significantly on exploring the methodological principles of TBLT in theory and practice (e.g., what TBLT means for language learning and assessment), and Constanza's on language-specific outworkings (e.g., what TBLT means for lesson and unit planning). On the one hand, and given Constanza's significant involvement in task-oriented teacher professional development (see Erlam & Tolosa, 2022), this move at the ITE level aimed to ensure that there would be greater synergy between the two components of the LTE programme. On the other hand, the change reinforced something of a polarisation between the two courses which exacerbated the constraints of the more strongly theoretical contribution of my own component (see Section 5.1.2).

The position of other teaching colleagues (e.g., the mentor ATs) in the promotion of innovation raises a further contextual constraint. For all the advocacy in its favour, TBLT has not been mandated in the New Zealand context. This thereby leaves the choice with regard to implementation down to individual teachers. Many established teachers in New Zealand do not teach according to task-based precepts, even if at times they may believe themselves to do so (see, e.g., East, 2012). More globally, there is persistent teacher uncertainty about what TBLT and tasks should look like in language classrooms (e.g., Long, 2016). The perceptions and perspectives of more experienced colleagues represent, as with the course tutors, a variable that was harder to control, and often there was little, if any, choice about where student teachers might end up on practicum.

5.2 To Innovate or Not to Innovate?

An elephant in the room, of course, is whether learner-centred and experiential innovations such as TBLT are the answer to enhancing L2 learning in classrooms.

Tobias and Duffy (2009) made clear that constructivism has exerted strong influence on educational thinking and practice over recent decades and has historical antecedents before this. On the other hand, they noted that there remain opponents as well as supporters of constructivist ideas and a constructivist-oriented approach to learning, and, as I noted earlier, there is contention in the literature around the efficacy of learner-centred vis-à-vis teacher-led. Indeed, Tobias and Duffy's edited volume represented one space in which oppositional ideas could be expressed. As they acknowledged, certainly a danger in these debates is that opponents 'too often talk past one another' (p. 6). Additionally, in Buttler's (2020) view, '[a] binary is often constructed between teacher-centered and student-centered teaching strategies that place traditional teaching behavior in opposition to constructivist teaching behavior' (p. 225). This perceptual binary can operate as a polarising force that attempts to push practitioners into one or the other camp.

When it comes to L2 pedagogy, one thing that theorists, researchers and practitioners do seem to be pretty universally agreed upon at this point in time is that classroom approaches need to promote the ability for L2 users ultimately to communicate authentically in real-world contexts. The communicative agenda is therefore mainstream.

My own experiences, both as a language learner and, subsequently, as a language user who needed to interact with others in different languages in a range of real-world contexts, had reinforced a belief in the primary goal of communicative competence. I brought this belief with me into my work as a teacher educator. In light of that belief, my engagement with a revised curriculum and the academic literature had led me to see TBLT as 'a potentially very powerful language pedagogy' (Van den Branden et al., 2009, p. 1).

However, as I reflected on course participants' own reflections and contributions to debates as they moved through the different stages of the ITE programme and grew in experience of working in schools and with other colleagues, I was compelled to grapple with a recurrent question – whether TBLT as innovation was in fact the most appropriate approach for New Zealand L2 classrooms.

It must be conceded that, within the overarching umbrella of so-called communicative competence, there is as yet no agreement about how best to teach and learn an L2. Certainly, strong advocates of TBLT would argue on the basis of empirical research findings that TBLT *is* the answer, portraying TBLT as potentially 'the long-awaited elixir of language teaching' (Richards & Rodgers, 2014, p. 177).

TBLT is, however, not without its critics. With particular regard to TBLT as innovation, even Long, a staunch advocate of TBLT, conceded, '[n]o approach to LT [language teaching] has proven "correct" to date' (Long, 2016, p. 28). More broadly, as Mitchell et al. (2019) put it, there can be 'no "one best method", however much research evidence supports it, which applies at all times and in all situations, with every type of learner' (p. 406). Innovations in practice must always be open to scrutiny, and eclecticism in practice (or at least an approach that accommodates the traditional within the innovative) may well be the most appropriate choice.

Furthermore, it is important to consider seriously the evidence arising from *teachers* about how innovation is going in practice. In the context of considering *in-service* teachers' encounters with TBLT in New Zealand, Erlam and Tolosa (2022) noted, 'TBLT theory needs to continue to engage with the realities of actual classroom practice, and to consider how this approach to language teaching may be maximally relevant to the different instructional contexts in which teachers are operating' (p. 252). More generally, Rose (2019) argued, 'theory development that revolves around teaching practices needs to involve teachers; and better still, be informed by teaching practices' (p. 898). Rose made the call for 'more teaching-informed research to disrupt the current unidirectional flow of knowledge between teachers and researchers' and 'encourage greater engagement of teachers and teacher educators in developing our knowledge base of language teaching' (p. 896). This approach, he argued, 'would better ensure real-world issues impacted by shifts in theoretical perspective are considered' (p. 899).

From a teacher education perspective, I ended up positioning myself as favouring a hybrid that sees TBLT as a development of, rather than a sweeping departure from, prior practices, one that encourages (even centralises) the use of tasks, but also one that can accommodate task use within more traditional teacher-fronted elements. Indeed, this hybrid is acknowledged in much of the TBLT literature as a viable, although less radical, interpretation of TBLT, and is sometimes labelled as task-*supported* language teaching. Ellis (2019) spoke of a modular approach that advocates the use of tasks but that allows for structured focus on grammatical form alongside their use. The position I have thus far reached on this is that the balanced perspectives ultimately taken by the teachers I worked with were a good thing. However, I must, as a teacher educator committed to my own reflective practice, remain open to the possibility that my perspective may shift as additional evidence comes to light.

5.3 Questions that Remain

Brandenberg and Jones (2017) asserted, 'reflection is an *ongoing* cycle of learning about one's teaching ... [that] does not necessarily resolve issues, but perhaps generates even more questions and problems' (p. 264, my emphasis). In the face of the range of contradictions I experienced, several questions remain. Firstly, and more generally:

- How should the exploration of innovations be enacted in teacher education programmes in light of arguments and counter-arguments about the innovation and its place in the wider discourse about effective teaching and learning – teacher-led versus learner-centred?
- Did I go far enough in explicitly modelling the innovation?
- What might explicit modelling of the innovation look like in a course that, due to its position within a broader academic programme, was required to lay a solid theoretical/methodological foundation?
- How might the exploration of theory/methodology become more innovative or learner-centred?

Secondly, and more specifically with regard to TBLT:

- To what extent did I weaken what TBLT as innovation *should* be in school classrooms by way of accommodation to contextual limitations?
- Did I go too far in accommodating beginning teacher anxiety and more experienced colleagues' ambivalence?
- Did I thereby *limit* beginning teachers' potential to transform the L2 learning experience of their students?

Or:

- Did I *adapt* my understanding to what TBLT as innovation *needs* to be in school classrooms by way of acknowledging that, in reality, there can be no 'one best method'?
- Did I thereby make TBLT's potential in time-limited instructional contexts real and manageable for beginning teachers?

It is important to me as a language teacher educator engaged in reflection on my own practices to remain open to Long's (2016) conclusion that '[a]dvances in theory and research, coupled with further field trials, will assuredly refine current models [of TBLT], and quite probably identify needed changes' (pp. 28–29). I view critical self-reflection, as documented here as an S-STEP, as an important tool in the process of raising questions and identifying shifts that might yet need to occur.

5.4 Implications for Language Teacher Education

With regard to my own approach to LTE, I draw the following conclusions from the data I collected: if, as teacher educators, we are to take new or inexperienced teachers with us on journeys into innovation, we need, first and foremost, to respect what these teachers already think, know and believe (Borg, 2003). We must listen attentively to their concerns and misgivings, before, during and after any process of innovation. We must be willing and open to what these concerns and misgivings might tell us about effective practice, and willing and open to modify our own beliefs (and practices) based on what they tell us. It is at this point in particular that language teacher educators must be prepared to reflect on their own work, both in practice and in research. Nonetheless, we as teacher educators must not shy away from challenging our own and others' current practices in light of theory and innovative ideas, and thereby throwing down the gauntlet for new and inexperienced teachers to take up. Several assurances about the directions I took can be found in the LTE/S-STEP literature.

Wright (2010) identified four elements that he saw as crucial to the enactment of successful LTE programmes:

1. Developing reflective practice
2. Exploring and challenging prior beliefs
3. Preparing teachers for the complexities of real classrooms
4. Including research-informed theory (pp. 266–267).

These elements are mirrored in what my own practices became as an ITE teacher educator, although I would tend to reorder these components. I would start with exploring prior beliefs. I would move on to including research-informed theory that might challenge prior beliefs. I would, on that basis, prepare teachers for future classroom experiences. As an overarching (or underpinning) goal, I would encourage the development of reflective practice. Thus, Wright begins with reflective practice, and I see reflective practice as an essential foundation.

With regard to effective LTE, Wright (2010) acknowledged a 'theoretical shift from behaviourism to constructivism' which has necessitated 'a recasting of the learning teacher from a "consumer" of received knowledge to a thinker, a practitioner who forms their own working theory' (pp. 266–267). This interpretation of constructivism in LTE provides an assurance about my own practices – my primary goal with the teachers I worked was that *they* should become thinking practitioners able to put together their own working theories (even when these working theories clashed with the innovation I was attempting to promote). The vignettes I presented exemplify how several of the teachers I worked with formulated their own theories about what was appropriate.

A key question for Buttler (2020) was, '[h]ow does a constructivist teacher impact the learning of students differently than a traditional teacher using a transmission model of teaching?' (p. 225). Drawing on a framework proposed by Brooks and Brooks (2001), Buttler outlined five elements that he believed were components of a constructivist-oriented approach to teacher education. From this perspective, constructivist teachers:

- seek out and value their students' standpoints
- challenge their students' beliefs
- encourage their students to see the relevance of the curriculum from a personal perspective
- organise their own input around primary concepts, rather than minutiae – what Brooks and Brooks (2001) labelled 'big ideas'
- provide input-embedded assessments that give students opportunities to connect in a personal way with their experiences.

Again, this interpretation of constructivism in LTE provides an assurance. If I consider my own practices retrospectively against this five-element framework, I can see that, in many respects, I sought to encourage this model.

In light of the changes to practice that I made between two comparative data collection points, 2012 and 2017, it is curious that, as I noted at the end of Section 4.5, there were no statistically significant differences between the two cohorts with regard to a quantitative comparison of frequency of comments regarding both advantages and drawbacks of TBLT (East, 2021b, p. 558). Notwithstanding the limitation in interpreting this due to the sample sizes, it would seem as if modifications to my own practices whereby the balances shifted somewhat between teacher-led moments and learner-centred activities, and whereby the presentation of TBLT ideas also shifted, did not in reality make any substantial difference to these beginning teachers' learning outcomes. Perhaps the important question about effectively reconciling the *guide on the side* with the *sage on the stage* is something of a red herring. Perhaps more important is that effective pedagogy (in both L2 classrooms and LTE programmes) includes and incorporates both elements – or the eclecticism in practice that each of the teacher vignettes I have presented alludes to – and that the balance between the two elements is not a defining factor for success (i.e., there is no one 'best method').

It must also be acknowledged (as I did at the end of Section 4.7 and as the vignettes in Section 4 also illustrated) that ITE is one small initial step on a much longer professional journey (Wright, 2010), and that the development of teachers' practices requires a considerable amount of time investment and a visiting and revisiting of ideas and concepts over several years. This is especially so if innovation is to be mediated successfully. Norris (2015) concluded that, when it comes to the success of implementing TBLT as innovation, 'teacher change takes time, requires individualized support that respects the teacher's agency, and must value the central mediating role played by the teacher in enabling instructional innovation in the first place' (p. 47).

Van den Branden (2009a) and Pachler et al. (2009) brought out clearly the long-term initiative that *teachers themselves* must take if innovation is to become more mainstream in L2 classroom practices. Van den Branden asserted that facilitating shifts in language teachers' beliefs and practices should be viewed as 'a *process* rather than an *event*' and 'an *unfolding* of experience and a *gradual development* of skill and sophistication in using the innovation' (p. 665, my emphases). Pachler et al. noted that becoming an effective L2 teacher 'requires a commitment ... to keep up with new developments in the field as well as ... willingness to engage in continuing professional development'. This may require explorations of pedagogical practices that may well 'challenge sometimes deeply held personal views' (p. 2).

This Element has only touched on the potential impact that PLD for in-service teachers can make in embedding innovation into teachers' practices. In East (2021b), I acknowledged nonetheless that, if we are to gain a broader picture of innovation and hindrances to it, a future focus of investigation should be practising and more experienced teachers. That is, 'it is feasible to conclude that the *practising teacher variable* is in need of attention moving forward' (p. 564, my emphasis).

5.5 Conclusion – Where to from Here?

As I noted towards the start of this Element, in one key aspect the work presented here has been an experiment, and experimentation entails some risk. I have attempted to apply an innovative methodological approach – S-STEP – to a matter about which I feel passionate and have collected a broad range of data. Despite Peercy and Sharkey's (2020) argument for its validity as a legitimate genre of research, initially through AERA's S-STEP SIG (see Section 2.3), S-STEP is an emerging field of educational enquiry, subject to a level of scepticism and 'noticeably absent from the major research venues in LTE' (p. 108). As I bring this Element to a close, it is important to address several limitations.

Firstly, the conclusions presented here might have been strengthened if I had engaged, right from the start, in formally documenting my own journey and reflections in an autobiographical or autoethnographic way. For example, comparing the vignettes I chose with the Personal Narratives that Barkhuizen (2019) drew on, it may be suggested that the vignettes I presented might have been more instructive if they had been my own real-time reflections at different points in time rather than the reflections of others. That said, and as I acknowledged earlier, the 2012 data were initially collected primarily to document the participants' voices. It was only as I began to analyse the data that I became more acutely aware of issues that required my attention as the teacher educator. These and subsequent data thus became the springboards for my own reflections.

Secondly, all of the participants whose stories I relied on to inform my reflections were, at one time or another, my own students. Bergmark et al. (2018) acknowledged, with regard to their own study, a possible weakness in this approach when they noted, 'the results can be criticised given that we have taught the courses and designed the assignments, which may have influenced the students to write responses that would be perceived as "politically correct"'.

They went on to argue, '[i]t seems, however, that the students expressed their views openly and in diverse ways' (p. 270). The evidence from my own longitudinal study, which enabled a level of data triangulation across several different sources, would suggest that the views expressed by the participants were, on the whole, genuine reflections of their own thinking and beliefs, and therefore valid springboards for my own subsequent reflections.

Fundamentally, an underlying perceptual challenge for S-STEP is that of validity or trustworthiness. In this regard, Hamilton et al. (2020) argued that trustworthiness in S-STEP must move beyond 'traditional notions of academic legitimacy' (p. 302). For them, trustworthiness:

- lies first and foremost in 'a responsibility lived out relationally with those [with] whom we live and work' (p. 300) – what we find out has implications for our own practices and this entails an ethical duty of care to those who will be most directly impacted
- also relies on 'an obligation to the unseen children we serve along with the colleagues and teachers who will read our work and learn from our experience' (p. 309) – there is an ethical duty of care to a broader range of stakeholders
- is evidenced by 'whether those that encounter the research find it trustworthy' (p. 308) and the 'resonance that other researchers experience as they read the work' (p. 313).

With regard to this last point, Bullough and Pinnegar (2001) suggested that valid or trustworthy autobiographical self-studies need to:

- ring true and enable connection
- promote insight and interpretation
- offer fresh perspectives on established truths
- provoke, challenge and illuminate rather than confirm and settle.

I hope that language teacher educators and others reading this Element will have found its conclusions trustworthy by virtue of resonance with their own experiences. That is, I hope that they will have found dimensions of this retrospective self-study with which they can connect in their own work and which act as a provocation, challenge and illumination in their own contexts. There are several key messages for teacher education practice which I trust will resonate with others, at whatever level of teacher education with which they are involved (pre-service, in-service, higher education). A focus on innovation:

- can successfully challenge and change existing beliefs
- can bring about successful changes to practice

- does not mean (and does not have to mean) the abandonment of all more traditional practices
- should occur in the context of ongoing teacher reflection to continually evaluate the success of the innovation in the face of evidence
- should be open to adjustments in light of the evidence of ongoing reflection.

Hamilton et al. (2020) also argued that, ultimately, trustworthy S-STEP research 'always turns back to self ... [and] what the study reveals to the teacher educator' (p. 317). That is, 'the purpose of the project, either explicitly and directly or implicitly and indirectly, must always be improvement of the practice of the researcher' (p. 330). My own attempt to apply an S-STEP research approach has been undertaken as a means to address what I see as a central question – how might I improve my own practice? The self-study presented here has enabled me to document shifts in my thinking, understanding and practice that I believe have contributed to successful learning outcomes for my students and a balanced and realistic approach to ITE practice. In retrospect, I believe I have learned a good deal, and also see potential for further growth and development.

For me, 2017 in fact marked the culmination of ten years in ITE. In my own professional life, I have now moved on from the work in the ITE space I present in this Element. The programme on which I now primarily teach is a masters level programme – the MTESOL – this time for teachers internationally who work principally (although not exclusively) beyond New Zealand. I now teach a dedicated course on TBLT, offered as an elective within the degree, and largely outside of the direct constraints of the New Zealand context. This course enables a connection with participants who come to the programme with a level of experience with teaching. Despite the shift from ITE, I remain a learner of LTE (Peercy & Sharkey, 2020) and continue to weigh the evidence and feedback I receive on my practices. Summative evaluative comments that I have received from students in the course over the few years that I have taught it indicate its potential to inspire innovative thinking. Comments I recorded in East (2021a) were:

- 'Task based teaching helped me to see another method of teaching language other than what I was already familiar with. It made me question how I was teaching and how I could make changes.'
- The course enabled 'a new view of teaching and learning.'
- This 'totally different approach for language learning stimulated my motivation.'
- The course 'expanded both my knowledge and my perceptions of education' (p. xiv).

Other comments have noted that the course:

- 'helped expand on my previous teaching experiences and will definitely inform me on my professional practices in future'
- 'has broadened my horizon on task-based language teaching.'

All the above comments speak clearly to augmented and deepened knowledge and understanding of innovation in L2 pedagogy. My approach nonetheless remains somewhat didactic in the context of a university that (at least up to the disruptions caused by COVID-19) has operated within a largely traditional format of course delivery. Inevitably, students also spoke of the ongoing need to consider *more* interaction in class, *more* opportunities to discuss ideas, *more* examples of tasks. Taken as sources of evidence in the context of S-STEP, these comments signal positive reception of my approach to promoting innovation, and underscore the reality that effective pedagogy should include and incorporate both elements – top-down and bottom-up.

My questions also raise implications for innovative approaches such as TBLT. Two books, a decade apart, perhaps evidence shifts in my own thinking about TBLT as a consequence of my reflective engagement with what was happening in my LTE courses.

My first book on TBLT (East, 2012) was critiqued in one review (Hadley, 2013) that pointed towards unquestioned idealism – TBLT was characterised as a 'major religion' and I was portrayed as 'a true believer' (p. 194), subject to 'rosy prognostication' and 'clear bias' (p. 195). Apparently, I was unable to see, or unwilling to accept, the realities of what happened in real classrooms. Several years later, I responded by saying that, on the contrary, I was 'very mindful of the difficulties teachers may encounter when implementing TBLT as innovation in real-world classrooms and time-limited instructional contexts' (East, 2017b, p. 413). In retrospect, my claim in East (2017b) about classroom realities was predicated on the kind of reflection I have documented in this Element. Perhaps my portrayal of TBLT back in 2012 had erred towards an idealistic view (or at least could be interpreted in that way).

In the Preface to my second book on TBLT (East, 2021a), I wrote that its contents emerged from my own background both as a language teacher educator and as a researcher. I explained that the book represented those aspects of TBLT that I have come to view as significant as I have worked with students in a variety of contexts. I went on to argue that, in particular, the book was shaped by my own reflections on TBLT as I have 'imparted knowledge to students, as students have taken that knowledge and tried out ideas with language learners in different contexts, and as they have shared with me and their peers the joys and struggles emerging from what they have experienced' (p. xiv).

East (2021a) is perhaps more pragmatic in its treatment of the phenomenon of TBLT than East (2012) may have been perceived to be. At the very least, the book demonstrates my continuing commitment to exploring and engaging with theory and practice around TBLT as innovation. Seen from the perspective of S-STEP, East (2021a), alongside the publications that have arisen from my longitudinal study into beginning teachers' perspectives, represents my own scholarly contribution to what Hamilton and Pinneger (2014) referred to as the refinement and evolution of emerging and evolving practices. As I noted earlier, this (in their words) includes 'new content knowledge, new understandings of learning, and new ways of teaching' (p. 139). I now use East (2021a) as the foundational text for the TBLT course I currently teach.

In conclusion, I return to the arguments with which I began this Element. When it comes to implementing innovative ideas in classrooms, teachers are crucial to the success of the educational endeavour. Furthermore, several scholars whose work I have cited in this Element have underscored the huge complexities involved in helping teachers to embrace innovation. The findings presented here lead to the encouraging conclusion that beginning teachers' practices *can* be enhanced with suitable mediation, and this is a beneficial outcome. That is, the status quo appears not to remain an option for teachers who are introduced to innovative thinking and practice in their ITE. That said, nor is a wholesale overthrowing of established ideas. It seems there will always be elements of tradition that continue to find expression. This is not, however, necessarily a pessimistic case of *plus ça change, plus c'est la même chose*. The evidence I have presented suggests that teachers' beliefs and practices can and do change when confronted with innovative ideas, albeit sometimes in small and incremental ways. Making changes to teaching and learning practices can be a tricky business, but it is not beyond the bounds of possibility.

References

Adamson, B., & Davison, C. (2003). Innovation in English language teaching in Hong Kong primary schools: One step forward, two steps sideways? *Prospect, 18*(1), 27–41.

Aitken, G., & Sinnema, C. (2008). *Effective Pedagogy in Social Sciences: Best Evidence Synthesis Iteration.* Wellington: Ministry of Education.

Barkhuizen, G. (2019). *Language Teacher Educator Identity.* Cambridge: Cambridge University Press.

Benson, P., & Voller, P. (Eds.). (1997). *Autonomy and Independence in Language Learning.* London: Longman.

Berben, M., Van den Branden, K., & Van Gorp, K. (2007). 'We'll see what happens': Tasks on paper and tasks in a multilingual classroom. In K. Van den Branden, K. Van Gorp, & M. Verhelst (Eds.), *Tasks in Action: Task-Based Language Education from a Classroom-Based Perspective* (pp. 32–67). Cambridge: Cambridge Scholars.

Beretta, A. (1986). *Evaluation of a Language-Teaching Project in South India.* University of Edinburgh PhD thesis.

Bergmark, B., Lundström, S., Manderstedt, L., & Palo, A. (2018). Why become a teacher? Student teachers' perceptions of the teaching profession and motives for career choice. *European Journal of Teacher Education, 41*(3), 266–281.

Blake, R. (2011). Current trends in online language learning. *Annual Review of Applied Linguistics, 31,* 19–35.

Borg, S. (2003). Teacher cognition in language teaching: A review of research on what language teachers think, know, believe, and do. *Language Teaching, 36,* 81–109.

Borg, S. (2011). The impact of in-service teacher education on language teachers' beliefs. *System, 39*(3), 370–380.

Borg, S. (2015). *Teacher Cognition and Language Education: Research and Practice.* London: Bloomsbury Academic.

Borg, S. (2019). Language teacher cognition: Perspectives and debates. In X. Gao (Ed.), *Second Handbook of English Language Teaching* (pp. 1149–1170). Cham: Springer.

Brandenberg, R., & Jones, M. (2017). Toward transformative reflective practice in teacher education. In R. Brandenberg, K. Glasswell, M. Jones, & J. Ryan (Eds.), *Reflective Theory and Practice on Teacher Education* (pp. 259–273). Singapore: Springer.

Braun, V., & Clarke, V. (2006). Using thematic analysis in psychology. *Qualitative Research in Psychology*, *3*(2), 77–101.

Brooks, J., & Brooks, M. (2001). *In Search of Understanding: The Case for Constructivist Classrooms* (3rd ed.). Hoboken: Prentice-Hall.

Brouwer, N., & Korthagen, F. (2005). Can teacher education make a difference? *American Educational Research Journal*, *42*(1), 153–224.

Brown, H. D. (2014). *Principles of Language Learning and Teaching* (6th ed.). New York: Pearson.

Bruner, J. S. (1960). *The Process of Education*. Cambridge, MA: Harvard University Press.

Bruner, J. S. (1966). *Towards a Theory of Instruction*. Cambridge, MA: Harvard University Press.

Bruner, J. S. (1973). *Going Beyond the Information Given*. New York: Norton.

Bullough, R. V., & Pinnegar, S. (2001). Guidelines for quality in autobiographical forms of self-study research. *Educational Researcher*, *30*(3), 13–21.

Burns, A. (2010). *Doing Action Research in English Language Teaching: A Guide for Practitioners*. New York: Routledge.

Buttler, T. (2020). Disrupting my teaching practices: A teacher educator living as a contradiction. *Studying Teacher Education*, *16*(2), 222–239.

Bygate, M. (2020). Some directions for the possible survival of TBLT as a real world project. *Language Teaching*, *53*(3), 275–288.

Cabaroglu, N., & Roberts, J. (2000). Development in student teachers' pre-existing beliefs during a 1-year PGCE programme. *System*, *28*, 387–402.

Carless, D. (2009). Revisiting the TBLT versus P-P-P debate: Voices from Hong Kong. *Asian Journal of English Language Teaching*, *19*, 49–66.

Carless, D. (2012). TBLT in EFL settings: Looking back and moving forward. In A. Shehadeh & C. Coombe (Eds.), *Task-Based Language Teaching in Foreign Language Contexts: Research and Implementation* (pp. 345–358). Amsterdam: John Benjamins.

Chinese Ministry of Education. (2011). *Chinese National English Curriculum*. Beijing: Normal University Publication Group.

Coe, R., Aloisi, C., Higgins, S., & Elliot Major, L. (2014). *What Makes Great Teaching? Review of the Underpinning Research*. London: The Sutton Trust.

Curriculum Development Council. (1997). *Syllabuses for Primary Schools: English Language (Primary 1–6)*. Hong Kong: Government Printer.

Curriculum Development Council. (1999). *Syllabuses for Secondary Schools: English Language (Secondary 1–5)*. Hong Kong: Government Printer.

Curriculum Development Council. (2002). *English Language Education Key Learning Area: Curriculum Guide (Primary 1–Secondary 3)*. Hong Kong: Government Printer.

Curriculum Development Council. (2007). *English Language Education Key Learning Area: English Language Curriculum and Assessment Guide (Secondary 4–6)*. Hong Kong: Government Printer.

Davis, S. (2005). Developing reflective practice in pre-service student teachers: What does art have to do with it? *Teacher Development, 9*(1), 9–19.

East, M. (2012). *Task-Based Language Teaching from the Teachers' Perspective: Insights from New Zealand*. Amsterdam: John Benjamins.

East, M. (2014). Encouraging innovation in a modern foreign language initial teacher education programme: What do beginning teachers make of task-based language teaching? *The Language Learning Journal, 42*(3), 261–274.

East, M. (2017a). Out with the old and in with the new? The benefits and challenges of task-based language teaching from one teacher's perspective. *Babel, 51*(1), 5–12.

East, M. (2017b). Research into practice: The task-based approach to instructed second language acquisition. *Language Teaching, 50*(3), 412–424.

East, M. (2018). How do beginning teachers conceptualise and enact tasks in school foreign language classrooms? In V. Samuda, M. Bygate, & K. Van den Branden (Eds.), *TBLT as a Researched Pedagogy* (pp. 23–50). Amsterdam: John Benjamins.

East, M. (2019a). Embedding innovation into school modern foreign languages programmes: Outcomes of two teachers' inquiries into their own practices. *The European Journal of Applied Linguistics and TEFL, 8*(2), 141–157.

East, M. (2019b). Sustaining innovation in school modern foreign languages programmes: Teachers' reflections on task-based language teaching three years after initial teacher education. *The Language Learning Journal, 47*(1), 105–115.

East, M. (2021a). *Foundational Principles of Task-Based Language Teaching*. New York: Routledge.

East, M. (2021b). Replication research: What do beginning teachers make of task-based language teaching? A comparative re-production of East (2014). *Language Teaching, 54*(4), 552–566.

East, M. (2022). Teacher preparation and support for task-based language teaching. In M. J. Ahmadian & M. Long (Eds.), *The Cambridge Handbook of Task-Based Language Teaching* (pp. 447–462). Cambridge: Cambridge University Press.

Ellis, R. (2018). *Reflections on Task-Based Language Teaching*. Bristol: Multilingual Matters.

Ellis, R. (2019). Towards a modular language curriculum for using tasks. *Language Teaching Research, 23*(4), 454–475.

Erlam, R., & Tolosa, C. (2022). *Pedagogical Realities of Implementing Task-Based Language Teaching*. Amsterdam: John Benjamins.

Farrell, T. (2021). *Reflective Practice in Language Teaching*. Cambridge: Cambridge University Press.

Grierson, A. L. (2010). Changing conceptions of effective teacher education: The journey of a novice teacher educator. *Studying Teacher Education*, *6*(1), 3–15.

Griffiths, C. (2012). Focus on the teacher. *ELT Journal*, *66*(4), 468–476.

Griffiths, C. (2021). What about the teacher? *Language Teaching, FirstView*, 1–13. https://doi.org/10.1017/S0261444821000100

Ha, X. V., & Murray, J. (2021). The impact of a professional development program on EFL teachers' beliefs about corrective feedback. *System*, *96*, 102405, 1–14.

Hadley, G. (2013). Review of Task-based Language Teaching from the Teachers' Perspective. *System*, *41*(1), 194–196.

Hamilton, M. L., Hutchinson, D., & Pinnegar, S. (2020). Quality, trustworthiness, and self-study research. In J. Kitchen, A. Berry, S. M. Bullock, A. R. Crowe, M. Taylor, H. Guðjónsdóttir, & L. Thomas (Eds.), *The International Handbook of Self-Study of Teaching and Teacher Education Practices* (2nd ed.) (pp. 299–338). Singapore: Springer.

Hamilton, M. L., & Pinnegar, S. (2014). Self-study of teacher education practices as a pedagogy for teacher educator professional development. In C. Craig & L. Orland-Barak (Eds.), *International Teacher Education: Promising Pedagogies (Part A). Advances in Research on Teaching* (pp. 137–152). Bradford: Emerald.

Hattie, J. (2012). *Visible Learning for Teachers*. New York: Routledge.

Hipkins, R. (2010). *Reshaping the Secondary School Curriculum: Building the Plane While Flying It? Findings from NZCER National Survey of Secondary Schools 2009*. Wellington: New Zealand Council for Educational Research.

Hmelo-Silver, C. E., Duncan, R. G., & Chinn, C. A. (2007). Scaffolding and achievement in problem-based and inquiry learning: A response to Kirschner, Sweller, and Clark (2006). *Educational Psychologist*, *42*(2), 99–107.

Howatt, A. P. R. (1984). *A History of English Language Teaching*. Oxford: Oxford University Press.

Hyland, K., & Wong, L. (2013). Introduction: Innovation and implementation of change. In K. Hyland & L. Wong (Eds.), *Innovation and Change in English Language Education* (pp. 1–10). New York: Routledge.

Jackson, D. (2022). *Task-Based Language Teaching*. Cambridge: Cambridge University Press.

Kayi-Aydar, H., Gao, X., Miller, E. R., Varghese, M., & Vitanova, G. (Eds.). (2019). *Theorizing and Analyzing Language Teacher Agency*. Bristol: Multilingual Matters.

Killion, J., & Todnem, G. (1991). A process of personal theory building. *Educational Leadership, 48*(6), 14–16.

Kirschner, P. A., Sweller, J., & Clark, R. E. (2006). Why minimal guidance during instruction does not work: An analysis of the failure of constructivist, discovery, problem-based, experiential, and inquiry-based teaching. *Educational Psychologist, 41*(2), 75–86.

Kosnik, C., & Beck, C. (2009). Teacher education for literacy teaching: Research at the personal, istitutional, and collective levels. In D. Tidwell, M. Heston, & L. Fitzgerald (Eds.), *Research Methods for the Self-Study of Practice* (pp. 213–229). Dordrecht: Springer.

Lai, C. (2015). Task-based language teaching in the Asian context: Where are we now and where are we going? In M. Thomas & H. Reinders (Eds.), *Contemporary Task-Based Language Teaching in Asia* (pp. 12–29). London: Bloomsbury.

Larsen-Freeman, D. (2015). Research into practice: Grammar learning and teaching. *Language Teaching, 48*(2), 263–280.

Lightbown, P., & Spada, N. (2006). *How Languages are Learned* (3rd ed.). Oxford: Oxford University Press.

Liu, Y., & Xiong, T. (2016). Situated task-based language teaching in Chinese colleges: Teacher education. *English Language Teaching, 9*(5), 22–32.

Long, M. (2016). In defense of tasks and TBLT: Nonissues and real issues. *Annual Review of Applied Linguistics, 36*, 5–33.

Loughran, J. (2005). Researching teaching about teaching: Self-study of teacher education practices. *Studying Teacher Education, 1*(1), 5–16.

Luo, S., & Xing, J. (2015). Teachers' perceived difficulty in implementing TBLT in China. In M. Thomas & H. Reinders (Eds.), *Contemporary Task-Based Language Teaching in Asia* (pp. 139–155). London: Bloomsbury.

Medgyes, P. (1986). Queries from a communicative teacher. *ELT Journal, 40*(2), 107–112.

Ministry of Education. (1993). *The New Zealand Curriculum Framework*. Wellington: Learning Media.

Ministry of Education. (1995a). *Chinese in the New Zealand Curriculum*. Wellington: Learning Media.

Ministry of Education. (1995b). *Spanish in the New Zealand Curriculum*. Wellington: Learning Media.

Ministry of Education. (2002a). *French in the New Zealand Curriculum*. Wellington: Learning Media.

Ministry of Education. (2002b). *German in the New Zealand Curriculum.* Wellington: Learning Media.

Ministry of Education. (2007). *The New Zealand Curriculum.* Wellington: Learning Media.

Ministry of Education. (2017). *What's New or Different?* http://seniorsecondary .tki.org.nz/Learning-languages/What-s-new-or-different#vocab

Ministry of Education. (2021). *Principles and Actions that Underpin Effective Teaching in Languages.* http://seniorsecondary.tki.org.nz/Learning-languages/Pedagogy/Principles-and-actions

Mitchell, R., Myles, F., & Marsden, E. (2019). *Second Language Learning Theories* (4th ed.). New York: Routledge.

Moser, M., Wei, T., & Brenner, D. (2020). Remote teaching during COVID-19: Implications from a national survey of language educators. *System, 97,* 102431, 1–15.

Norris, J. (2015). Thinking and acting programmatically in task-based language teaching: Essential roles for programme evaluation. In M. Bygate (Ed.), *Domains and Directions in the Development of TBLT: A Decade of Plenaries from the International Conference* (pp. 27–57). Amsterdam: John Benjamins.

Norris, J., Bygate, M., & Van den Branden, K. (2009). Introducing task-based language teaching. In K. Van den Branden, M. Bygate, & J. Norris (Eds.), *Task-Based Language Teaching: A Reader* (pp. 15–19). Amsterdam: John Benjamins.

Norris, J., & Ortega, L. (2006). The value and practice of research synthesis for language learning and teaching. In J. Norris & L. Ortega (Eds.), *Synthesizing Research on Language Learning and Teaching* (pp. 1–50). Amsterdam: John Benjamins.

Pachler, N., Barnes, A., & Field, K. (2009). *Learning to Teach Modern Foreign Languages in the Secondary School* (3rd ed.). New York: Routledge.

Peercy, M. M., & Sharkey, J. (2020). Missing a S-STEP? How self-study of teacher education practice can support the language teacher education knowledge base. *Language Teaching Research, 24*(1), 105–115.

Peercy, M. M., Sharkey, J., Baecher, L., Motha, S., & Varghese, M. (2019). Exploring TESOL teacher educators as learners and reflective scholars: A shared narrative inquiry. *TESOL Journal, 10*(4), 1–16.

Perryman, J., & Calvert, G. (2020). What motivates people to teach, and why do they leave? Accountability, performativity and teacher retention. *British Journal of Educational Studies, 68*(1), 3–23.

Porte, G. (2013). Who needs replication? *The CALICO Journal, 30*(1), 10–15.

Porte, G., & McManus, K. (2019). *Doing Replication Research in Applied Linguistics*. New York: Routledge.

Prabhu, N. (1987). *Second Language Pedagogy*. Oxford: Oxford University Press.

Prabhu, N. S. (1982). *The Communicational Teaching Project, South India*. Madras: The British Council.

Richards, J. C., Ho, B., & Giblin, K. (1996). Learning how to teach in the RSA Certificate. In D. Freeman & J. C. Richards (Eds.), *Teacher Learning in Language Teaching* (pp. 242–259). Cambridge: Cambridge University Press.

Richards, J. C., & Rodgers, T. S. (2014). *Approaches and Methods in Language Teaching* (3rd ed.). Cambridge: Cambridge University Press.

Rose, H. (2019). Dismantling the ivory tower in TESOL: A renewed call for teaching-informed research. *TESOL Quarterly, 53*(3), 895–905.

Ruan, J., & Leung, C. B. (2012). Introduction. In J. Ruan & C. B. Leung (Eds.), *Perspectives on Teaching and Learning English Literacy in China* (pp. ix–xii). Dordrecht: Springer.

Samuda, V. (2005). Leading from behind: A role for task design awareness. Symposium: The role of the teacher in TBLT. 1st International Conference on Task-Based Language Teaching, *From Theory to Practice*, September 21–23, Leuven, Belgium.

Savignon, S. (2018). Communicative competence. In J. I. Liontas (Ed.), *The TESOL Encyclopedia of English Language Teaching* (pp. 1–7). Hoboken, NJ: John Wiley & Sons.

Schmidt, H. G., Loyens, S. M. M., Van Gog, T., & Paas, F. (2007). Problem-Based Learning *is* compatible with human cognitive architecture: Commentary on Kirschner, Sweller, and Clark (2006). *Educational Psychologist, 42*(2), 91–97.

Schön, D. A. (1983). *The Reflective Practitioner: How Professionals Think in Action*. New York: Basic Books.

Schön, D. A. (1987). *Educating the Reflective Practitioner: Toward a New Design For Teaching and Learning in the Professions*. San Fransisco, CA: Jossey-Bass.

Schweisfurth, M. (2013). *Learner-Centred Education in International Perspective: Whose Pedagogy for Whose Development?* New York: Routledge.

Snyder, R. (2017). Resistance to change among veteran teachers: Providing voice for more effective engagement. *National Council of Professors of Educational Administration International Journal of Educational Leadership Preparation, 12*(1), 1–14.

Strickler, U. (2022). *Technology and Language Teaching*. Cambridge: Cambridge University Press.

Thomas, N., & Brereton, P. (2019). Practitioners respond to Michael Swan's 'Applied Linguistics: A consumer's view'. *Language Teaching, 52*(2), 275–278.

Tidwell, D., Heston, M., & Fitzgerald, L. (2009). Introduction. In D. Tidwell, M. Heston, & L. Fitzgerald (Eds.), *Research Methods for the Self-Study of Practice* (pp. xiii–xxii). Dordrecht: Springer.

Tobias, S., & Duffy, T. (Eds.). (2009). *Constructivist Instruction: Success or Failure?* New York: Routledge.

Tocci, C., Ryan, A. M., & Pigott, T. D. (2019). Changing teaching practice in P–20 educational settings: Introduction to the Volume. *Review of Research in Education, 43*(1), vii–xiii.

Tran, N. G., Ha, X. V., & Tran, N. H. (2021). EFL reformed curriculum in Vietnam: An understanding of teachers' cognitions and classroom practices. *RELC Journal*, OnlineFirst, pp. 1–17.

Ur, P. (2012). *A Course in English Language Teaching*. Cambridge: Cambridge University Press.

Van den Branden, K. (2006). Introduction: Task-based language teaching in a nutshell. In K. Van den Branden (Ed.), *Task-Based Language Education: From Theory to Practice* (pp. 1–16). Cambridge: Cambridge University Press.

Van den Branden, K. (2009a). Diffusion and implementation of innovations. In M. Long & C. Doughty (Eds.), *The Handbook of Language Teaching* (pp. 659–672). Chichester: Wiley Blackwell.

Van den Branden, K. (2009b). Mediating between predetermined order and chaos: The role of the teacher in task-based language education. *International Journal of Applied Linguistics, 19*(3), 264–285.

Van den Branden, K. (2016). The role of teachers in task-based language education. *Annual Review of Applied Linguistics, 36*, 164–181.

Van den Branden, K. (2022a). *How to Teach an Additional Language: To Task or Not to Task?* Amsterdam: John Benjamins.

Van den Branden, K. (2022b). TBLT as an innovation: A task for teachers. In M. J. Ahmadian and M. Long (Eds.). *The Cambridge Handbook of Task-Based Language Teaching* (pp. 628–648). Cambridge: Cambridge University Press.

Van den Branden, K., Bygate, M., & Norris, J. (2009). Task-based language teaching: Introducing the reader. In K. Van den Branden, M. Bygate, & J. Norris (Eds.), *Task-Based Language Teaching: A Reader* (pp. 1–13). Amsterdam: John Benjamins.

Weimer, M. (2013). *Learner-Centered Teaching: Five Key Changes to Practice* (2nd, Ed.). San Fransisco, CA: Jossey Bass.

Widdowson, H. G. (1993). Innovation in teacher development. *Annual Review of Applied Linguistics, 13*, 260–275.

Williams, R., & Grudnoff, L. (2011). Making sense of reflection: A comparison of beginning and experienced teachers' perceptions of reflection for practice. *Reflective Practice: International and Multidisciplinary Perspectives, 12*(3), 281–291.

Willis, J. (1996). *A Framework for Task-Based Learning*. London: Longman Pearson Education. Available from: https://www.intrinsicbooks.co.uk/titles/framework.html

Wright, T. (2010). Second language teacher education: Review of recent research on practice. *Language Teaching, 43*(3), 259–296.

Xiongyong, C., & Samuel, M. (2011). Perceptions and implementation of task-based language teaching among secondary school EFL teachers in China. *International Journal of Business and Social Science, 2*(24), 292–302.

Zeichner, K. M. (1999). The new scholarship in teacher education. *Educational Researcher, 28*(9), 4–15.

Zeichner, K. M., & Tabachnick, B. R. (1981). Are the effects of university teacher education "washed out" by school experience? *Journal of Teacher Education, 32*(3), 7–13.

Zhang, Y. (2007). TBLT innovation in primary school English language teaching in mainland China. In K. Van den Branden, K. Van Gorp, & M. Verhelst (Eds.), *Tasks in Action: Task Based Language Education from a Classroom-Based Perspective* (pp. 68–91). Cambridge: Cambridge Scholars Press.

Zheng, X., & Borg, S. (2014). Task-based learning and teaching in China: Secondary school teachers' beliefs and practices. *Language Teaching Research, 18*(2), 205–221.

Cambridge Elements ≡

Language Teaching

Heath Rose
Linacre College, University of Oxford

Heath Rose is an Associate Professor of Applied Linguistics at the University of Oxford. At Oxford, he is course director of the MSc in Applied Linguistics for Language Teaching. Before moving into academia, Heath worked as a language teacher in Australia and Japan in both school and university contexts. He is author of numerous books, such as *Introducing Global Englishes*, *The Japanese Writing System*, *Data Collection Research Methods in Applied Linguistics*, and *Global Englishes for Language Teaching*. Heath's research interests are firmly situated within the field of second language teaching, and includes work on Global Englishes, teaching English as an international language, and English Medium Instruction.

Jim McKinley
University College London

Jim McKinley is an Associate Professor of Applied Linguistics and TESOL at UCL, Institute of Education, where he serves as Academic Head of Learning and Teaching. His major research areas are second language writing in global contexts, the internationalisation of higher education, and the relationship between teaching and research. Jim has edited or authored numerous books including the *Routledge Handbook of Research Methods in Applied Linguistics*, *Data Collection Research Methods in Applied Linguistics*, and *Doing Research in Applied Linguistics*. He is also an editor of the journal, *System*. Before moving into academia, Jim taught in a range of diverse contexts including the US, Australia, Japan and Uganda.

Advisory Board

About the Series

This Elements series aims to close the gap between researchers and practitioners by allying research with language teaching practices, in its exploration of research-informed teaching, and teaching-informed research. The series builds upon a rich history of pedagogical research in its exploration of new insights within the field of language teaching.

Cambridge Elements $\equiv$

Language Teaching

Printed in the United States
by Baker & Taylor Publisher Services